Teammate Tuesdays

A Year of Good Teammate Musings

LANCE LOYA

CAGER HAUS
PUBLISHING

ISBN-13: 978-1-7325505-0-6

www.coachloya.com

Design and publishing by Cager Haus.
Cover image by Kutsal Lenger, Dreamstime.com.

For Laken and Lakota…may you always be good teammates.

Contents

Acknowledgements

A special thank you to Wendy Clouner for suggesting that I start a blog. Although I wasn't initially receptive to your suggestion, I am glad I eventually acquiesced. I also want to express my gratitude to Rachel Loya, Cindy Davis, and Craig Sikurinec for your continued support and recommendations.

Introduction

What does it really mean to be a good teammate?

Not long ago, I set out on a journey to discover an answer to that question.

In many ways, the journey began with the publication of my children's book *Be a Good Teammate*. I initially wrote that book for my two young daughters. However, it unexpectedly set into motion a sequence of events that led to my belief that the world needs more good teammates—kind, unselfish individuals who put the needs of their "team" ahead of their own agendas.

The children's book revolved around the thought that good teammates do three things: care, share, and listen. My desire to expand on that thought led to the next stage of the journey—my second book, the nonfiction title *Building Good Teammates: The Story of My Mount Rushmore, a Coaching Epiphany, and That Nun*. It was basically an adult version of the children's book that explained why being a good teammate should be taught and emphasized in amateur sports.

Eventually, I reached a point in my journey where exploring the art of being a good teammate became my passion and my purpose. My ultimate goal was to share what I had discovered about what it really means to be a good teammate through a third, more comprehensive book.

While I was working on that book, someone suggested to me that writing a blog concurrently would be a great way to share some of the interesting thoughts I had along the way—my musings.

I took that person's advice and begin writing a blog, posting every Tuesday morning. I called the blog "Teammate Tuesdays." This book is a compilation of the posts from the entire first year of my blog.

I didn't intend for the posts to be compiled in this manner when I wrote them. That's worth noting, because this book doesn't follow the writing style of a traditional book. I tried not to alter the posts from the way they were originally published online. Sometimes, that translates into me doing things like repeating certain words and phrases in consecutive chapters. An editor wouldn't allow that to happen in a traditional book. However, I suspect it won't take much effort on your part to see past minor faux pas of that nature.

Although I didn't intend for the blog to become a book, I do like the idea of assembling an entire year's worth of posts in this form. The posts are worth sharing in an alternative medium. Not everyone who can benefit from hearing the message reads online blogs. Some people still like to hold a physical book in their hands. Putting the blog in book form makes it possible to share the message with a broader audience and to even give the blog as a gift.

A book is also a convenient way to bring those of you who may be joining the Good Teammate movement "already in progress" up to speed. The format allows you, as the reader, to experience your own journey of discovery, at your own pace. You don't have to wait until the next week to see what I am going to write about in my blog. You can read the posts as fast or slow as you desire. It is like binge watching a blog.

So why Tuesdays?

In my experience, Tuesdays are generally the best days for personal and professional development.

Wednesdays mark the middle of the week. You've come to the realization that you better put your nose to the grindstone and get busy before the week ends, or you're going to run out of time.

Thursdays still have some of the same urgency to get your work done as the previous day. But by Thursday afternoon, you are starting to set your sights on the weekend.

Fridays are the day to wrap up loose ends and then coast through the rest of the day. It's the end of the work week, so you're reluctant to start any new projects. You may also feel a little burned out by Friday, and not necessarily motivated to engage in anything mentally taxing.

Saturdays are of course...Saturdays! It's the day to do chores around your house, like mowing your lawn and trimming your hedges. It's additionally a day for recreation and seeking fun.

Sundays are family time. You're ready to just relax and spend some quality time with your family. In the event that you don't love your job, you'll probably spend Sunday evenings stressing about having to go back to work the next day. Not much work gets done on Sundays.

Mondays are spent playing catch up. You're trying to finish all the work you didn't complete—but should have—last week. You seem to have a gazillion pressing emails and phone calls to return. By the time Mondays are over, you are exhausted.

Which brings us to Tuesdays. You are still a little tired from playing catch up on Monday and not anxious to put in another intense day of work. You also somehow manage to convince yourself that you have all week to get your work done. Tuesdays are the perfect day to read blogs and perhaps invest in a little self-improvement.

Sound familiar?

If so, then you've come to the right place. Every day is Tuesday in this book.

I hope you enjoy my collection of good teammate musings. My wish is for them to inspire you to be become a better version of yourself and equip you to help others do the same.

A New Adventure
APRIL 28

So, I am officially embarking on a new adventure and joining the world of blogging. And…this is officially my inaugural entry!

Which raises an obvious question: Who will benefit from reading my blog? Simple answer: Anybody. Better answer: Everybody. Why?

Because EVERYBODY is part of a team in some capacity. Unfortunately, this is a fact that often seems to escape us. Nevertheless, it is very much true.

If you are involved in sports, it is easy to see yourself as being part of a team. But there are all kinds of teams besides just sports teams.

A classroom is a team. A school is a team. A community is a team. The company where you work is a team. And, of course, a family is a team.

As a member of a team, you should have a desire to be the best teammate you can be.

I have come to realize that every affliction affecting our society today—school bullying, domestic violence, the drug epidemic, political shenanigans, etc.—comes down to people not being good teammates.

Quite frequently, those problems are just a matter of individuals not recognizing that they are part of a team, and failing to grasp that, as such, their choices have a ripple effect on everyone around them, i.e. their teammates.

The goal of my blog is twofold. First, to help inspire you to be a better teammate. Second, to help you find ways to inspire those on your team to be better teammates.

Inspire being the optimum word. I want to provide you with the sort of stories and observations that compel change. After all, inspiration is the spark that ignites all great revolutions.

Let's be honest, it can be difficult to directly confront a fellow teammate with a concern you have about the choices they are making, and the impact their choices are having on you and their other teammates. I hope my blog will give you another opportunity to do just that, by allowing my words to speak for you.

If you've made it this far and are still reading, then I want to express my sincere gratitude and say thank you. I think you are going to enjoy the ride.

I also want to give you the opportunity right now to start being a better teammate with a simple call to action:

Invest in yourself and go to *http://www.coachloya.com/blog-sign-up/* to subscribe to my blog. And…share this message with your teammates and ask them to subscribe, too.

Good teammates share, right?

With that, I will leave you with the signature signoff of my new blog…

Good teammates care. Good teammates share. Good teammates listen. Go be a good teammate.

When Teammates Share, They Inspire
MAY 9

Explaining the concept of sharing to elementary students can be a tall order. Whenever I speak at schools, I try to get kids to understand the breadth of what it means to share. They typically struggle with the idea that people can share more than just their possessions.

Right now, every elementary teacher—and anyone who is a parent of a child that has siblings—is smirking, because they know exactly how tall of an order it can be to get kids to share their toys. Imagine the difficulty of convincing kids they need to share more than just their toys in order to be a good teammate!

Nevertheless, that is exactly what must happen.

Good teammates certainly have a willingness to share their possessions, but they also need to have a willingness to share intangibles like their time, their knowledge, and their talents.

Interestingly, whenever I speak at corporate events, the necessity to share these intangibles is a concept that the adults often struggle to accept. They are protective of their personal life and reluctant to drop their guard long enough to engage in this type of sharing.

Which brings me to the story of Colin's 30-day challenge.

I first met Colin while playing basketball overseas. At the time, he was slightly older than most of the other members of our team, and served in the capacity of player/coach.

I found him to be inspirational in both of those roles.

Colin was almost always the smallest player on the court. Yet despite his age and his lack of height, he was routinely our team's leading rebounder. This was no minor feat, and undoubtedly due to his unmatched level of energy.

I lost touch with Colin over the years, but through the wonders of social media, I was recently able to reconnect with him.

It was through this medium that he threw down a challenge to his friends.

Colin had suffered a brain hemorrhage that nearly took his life. To commemorate the one-year anniversary of surviving his life altering event, he committed to forming a new habit and decided to run at least three miles every day for the next thirty days.

When he completed thirty days, he just kept going. Eventually, he reached 163 consecutive days. This is when he issued his challenge.

Colin announced that his new goal was to reach 200 consecutive days—a number that would coincide with his 50th birthday. He planned to complete this final run in Rome, Italy, at the top of the world famous Spanish Steps.

On day 163, Colin asked his friends to take the week and come up with an activity to do for the next 30 days, and then join him the following week in the final stage of his journey. The activity could be anything (playing a musical instrument, learning a new language, knitting, etc.), with the only caveat being the activity had to occupy a minimum of 30 minutes each day and had to be done for 30 straight days.

I accepted and decided to commit to logging 10,000 steps every day. (*FYI...I set my Fitbit my stride length to equal one meter, which works out to be a 10k meters per day.)

Like Colin, when 30 days arrived, I kept going...and have continued to do so each and every day since. I am now to the point where the thought of not completing this daily activity is incomprehensible.

Along the way, I lost a few unwanted pounds and experienced a genuine improvement in my overall health. However, just as Colin did, I also found myself more surprised by the ancillary benefits of making this commitment.

He stated what he noticed the most was how much mental strength he gained, knowing that he made himself run even when he really did not want to do so. Me too.

It was not always easy. I battled snow and rain, and even saw the task through to completion sometimes in airport terminals and hotel hallways. But I stuck with it...and I formed a new positive habit in the process.

The added bonus for me was that I got some of my best thinking done during those 10,000 steps. As some of you are aware, I am in the midst of putting together my next book, and I came up with some great ideas as a direct result of the time I invested in my commitment.

When Colin finished on day 200 at the top of the Spanish Steps, he had a run a total of 788 miles—the equivalent of 30 marathons.

He is a remarkable man, and a living example of one of the primary tenets of being a good teammate: When your individual efforts inspire others, you are a good teammate.

Colin's willingness to "put himself out there" and publicly share his experience inspired me. And now, I hope it inspires you. What activity can you commit to that will positively impact you and your team? I assure you, 30 days will go by quicker than you can imagine. But don't be surprised if when they do, you also *just keep going.*

As always, remember: Good teammates care. Good teammates share. Good teammates listen. Go be a good teammate.

(P.S. Colin, wherever you are today…thank you for being a good teammate and thank you for sharing.)

Defining Loyalty and Mama's Bowling Night
MAY 16

In many ways, an individual's capacity to be a good teammate is directly proportional to his or her ability to define loyalty.

I used to think loyalty was about being a good follower. I thought it was about finding someone or something you believed in and then settling into a supportive role.

But that's not real loyalty. That is the kind of loyalty that disappears the moment you realize that you are not following the right person, or that your loyalty is not being reciprocated. It's not the kind of loyalty that leads to an individual being a good teammate.

When I think of what it means to be loyal, I now think about *Mama's bowling night.* Let me explain.

Several years ago, I worked with someone who loved to go bowling. She was an extremely kind and friendly person. Everybody in the office loved her. In fact, the closest thing she had to an actual flaw was her unusual obsession with bowling.

Every Wednesday, she participated in a competitive bowling league. She unapologetically planned her life around that league. It got to the point that she even avoided doing things like typing on her keyboard on Wednesday afternoons, so her wrist could be "rested" for bowling later that night.

At the time, this woman had an incredibly cute, preschool-aged daughter, who understood her mother's bowling obsession better than anyone.

One day I asked the daughter if she was going to come to my team's next game, which happened to be on a Wednesday night. Her response was priceless and made everyone laugh:

"I can't. It's Mama's bowling night."

Her response became a running joke, with me attempting to up the ante every time I saw her. I would offer to take her for ice cream if she came to the game.

"I can't. It's Mama's bowling night."

I would offer to take her to Chuck E. Cheese's if she came to the game. Same response.

"I can't. It's Mama's bowling night."

I even offered—tongue in cheek—to take her to Disney World if she came to the game. But she always gave the same response.

"I can't. It's Mama's bowling night."

Her mother loved bowling and it was very clear that family decisions revolved around *Mama's bowling night.*

Eventually, the woman moved onto a different department and we no longer crossed paths on a daily basis. One afternoon, though, I happened to bump into her and I asked her how bowling was going.

She told me she didn't go bowling anymore. She had given it up.

I was shocked by her reply! I could not imagine her ever willingly giving up on bowling.

She went on to tell me how her daughter—now a fourth grader—was struggling in math. Her daughter's teacher gave the class a math test every Thursday. They had to pass the test, or they didn't get the reward of extra recess on Friday with the other kids.

Instead of going bowling, the women now spent Wednesday nights tirelessly giving practice math problems to her daughter.

This woman was able to do what, sadly, many people do not: *Prioritize their teams*. She loved going bowling and having fun with her bowling teammates. But she made a commitment to her other team too—her family. In this case, her commitment to her daughter's education was more important than her love for bowling.

Being loyal is primarily about prioritizing your teams and honoring your commitments. It's about making the necessary sacrifices to keep your commitments.

Ideally, loyalty is reciprocated…but there is no guarantee that it will be. Good teammates make a commitment and a choice to be loyal to their commitment. They do it because they care about their team, not because of some benefit that may or may not be returned in their favor. The reciprocation is not important to them. The commitment is.

By prioritizing your teams, you allow yourself clarity when you have to make difficult decisions.

The next time you find yourself in a situation where you need to make a choice, prioritize teams and be loyal to your commitment. And…think about *Mama's bowling night*.

As always, remember: Good teammates care. Good teammates share. Good teammates listen. Go be a good teammate.

The Duck Poster: Lead. Follow.
Or, Get Out of the Way
MAY 23

One of my wife's favorite childhood memories is of the day
she accompanied her father to a meeting in the state capital.

Her father was the supervisor of a state park and was
occasionally required to travel to the Capitol for official
business.

As he paraded his precocious daughter through the offices
on this particular day, introducing her to his colleagues, he
grew increasingly humored by how charming the six-year old
seemed to be towards the adults.

At some point during the visit, my wife commented to a
man that she really liked the poster hanging in his office. It
was a photo of a group of disorganized ducks, with the
caption "Lead. Follow. Or, Get out of the way."

Upon hearing of her fondness for the poster, the man
promptly removed it from his wall and gave it to the cute
little girl to take home with her.

That duck poster hung in her bedroom throughout her

childhood. It hung in her dormitory throughout her college years. And it hung in her crammed apartment throughout her twentysomething years.

Although time had caused the poster to become frayed and faded, it continued to offer my wife sound life advice: *Lead. Follow. Or, get out of the way.*

Before we were married, I remember seeing that poster whenever I came to visit and reading the caption.

It's a catchy, iconic phrase that has been around for generations. It's been used in presidential debates and in the titles of autobiographies. A quick Google search credits the quote to everybody from Thomas Paine to General George Patton to Ted Turner. The truth is no one can really seem to pin down exactly who first uttered those words.

As I dive deeper into the *Be a Good Teammate* mindset, though, the essence of the duck poster message has taken on new relevance for me.

I've learned that there is no consistent role into which a good teammate must fall. In fact, the spirit of being a good teammate is about your ability to adapt your role to team circumstances.

There are times when you need to lead. You have an obligation to the team to step up and take action. Maybe it is to provide direction to your teammates. Maybe it is to confront a source of toxicity within the team. But there are times when you need to have the courage to lead.

There are also times when you need to follow. Second-guessing decisions and questioning authority will eventually undermine the team's potential for achievement. Sometimes being a good teammate means you need to get beyond your own opinions and get onboard with what is best for the *team*. That means having the humility to follow.

And then there are those times when you don't know whether to lead or follow. In those moments, you need to have the courage, the humility, *and* the wisdom to simply get out of the way. You cannot allow your paralysis by analysis to hinder your team's progress.

Everyone on the team has a different role. However, every role is important and every role affects the team's capacity to succeed. Based on the circumstances of the situation, your role can change at any given moment.

Don't resist the change. Adapt. *Lead. Follow. Or, get out of the way.*

I don't know what ever became of the man who generously parted ways with his duck poster. But I can tell you that giving it to that charming six-year old was a *good teammate move* on his part—a move that most certainly had an impact on her life…my life…and now your life.

As always, remember: Good teammates care. Good teammates share. Good teammates listen. Go be a good teammate.

Remembering the Sacrifices of Good Teammates

MAY 30

America celebrated Memorial Day this past weekend, where we paid tribute to all who served and died in battle.

While Memorial Day has come to symbolize the unofficial start of summer, it's true meaning amazingly never really seems to get lost.

The holiday, originally known as Decoration Day, was initially an occasion for people to decorate the graves of both Union and Confederate soldiers who lost their lives during the Civil War.

The idea was to honor the fallen, regardless of what side they were on or what uniform they wore. It was an opportunity to recognize their *sacrifice*.

As I drove in my car yesterday, I heard the word sacrifice mentioned time and time again in radio commercials, as in, "Wishing you a safe and happy Memorial Day holiday and saying thank you to all of our military personnel who made the ultimate sacrifice."

People still appreciate the sacrifice associated with Memorial Day.

Recently, I was at a book festival promoting my books, when I met a man who shared the most fascinating story with me about a group of World War II soldiers.

As he approached my table, I asked him if he knew of any good teammates—a question I often ask of people I meet. His response was a little different than what I typically get.

The man, probably in his early sixties, said, "Yes, sir. The Wereth Eleven."

My interest was piqued.

For the next several minutes he recounted to me the story of the sacrifice of the Wereth Eleven.

During the Battle of the Bulge in December 1944, the Germans attacked the 106th Division near the Belgium-German border. Supporting the 106th Division was the 333rd Field Artillery Battalion, an all-black unit.

The 106th Division was overwhelmed in what would be one of the worst defeats suffered by Allied forces during the entire war. Most of the 333rd were killed during the battle. However, eleven of the soldiers from that unit were able to escape.

They walked through miles of deep snow until they came upon the small Belgium hamlet of Wereth. There a family took them into their home and gave them warm food and shelter. It was a dangerous move for the family to harbor the Americans.

When the Nazis eventually arrived at Wereth, the eleven soldiers vowed to protect the Belgium family who had extended kindness towards them. Sadly, however, their surrender was not accepted and they were brutally tortured and killed by the Germans.

The story of the Wereth Eleven would go untold for nearly 50 years, until a man named Hermann Langer made it his life's mission to see that the truth of the war crimes committed against the eleven soldiers was brought to light.

You see, Hermann was the 12-year old son of the Belgium man who offered shelter to the eleven soldiers on that cold December day in 1944.

He never forgot the sacrifice the soldiers made for his family. Had they been too cowardly to face the fate that awaited them and not surrendered, the Germans would have most certainly killed the entire family who harbored them.

You would be challenged to make an argument that our military personnel are anything but good teammates. They make a tremendous sacrifice every day, so that the rest of us—their teammates—can have freedom.

That is what good teammates do. They make sacrifices.

The hard part is that sometimes it seems that those sacrifices go unappreciated or even unnoticed. But that shouldn't make a difference. Good teammates don't make *good teammate moves* (like sacrifices) because they have an expectation of receiving the beneficiary's gratitude. They make them because it is the right thing to do and because it is best for the team.

If you enjoyed your Memorial Day weekend, then make an effort to find a way to honor someone who made a sacrifice for you by paying it forward and making a no-strings-attached sacrifice for someone else.

As always, remember: Good teammates care. Good teammates share. Good teammates listen. Go be a good teammate.

(*Learn more about the Wereth Eleven at *http://www.wereth.org/en/history*)

When Teachers Are Teammates
JUNE 6

As another school year comes to an end, I want to take a moment to recognize the many great teachers who are selflessly serving the educational needs of our youth.

My wife and I have been genuinely blessed the past few years in terms of the quality of teachers our daughters have had—and that is no understatement! Both of their teachers have been recognized as the school district's *Teacher of the Year*. We feel like we hit the "teacher lottery" and cannot even begin to express how grateful we are to have crossed paths with these fantastic educators.

When I think about my daughters' teachers, and some of the favorite teachers I had as a student, I cannot help but think about how much they cared.

Isn't that how people always reply when asked what made a particular teacher in their life so special? The response is *always*, "They really cared about me."

Caring is a hallmark of a good teammate, and all of the aforementioned teachers inevitably see themselves as being a teammate in the educational process.

They are fully invested in their commitment to their student, which solidifies their loyalty to the student. They see their student's success as their success, and their student's failure as their failure.

They communicate and solicit feedback from the student and their parents. They want to know what more they can do to help, and they don't treat the process as a one-way endeavor.

The idea of being inconvenienced by the process is simply a nonfactor to them.

Having worked in higher education for many years, I have seen more than a few professors during that time who frustrated me with their approach to the classroom.

It drove me nuts whenever I saw an instructor hand out the syllabus, layout the reading assignments, give the date of the exam, and then top it off with the infamous words *"everything you need to know is in the book."*

That is not sound teaching, and those are not the words and actions of a teacher who cares.

A teacher with that kind of approach is putting the learning onus solely on the student. If the student fails, then it is supposedly the student's own fault.

When teachers see themselves as being a teammate, they attack a student's failure from a different angle. They use their creativity to come up with an alternative way to get the student to learn the information. And they keep coming up with alternative ways until it is learned.

Last fall—although it seems like it just happened yesterday—I walked my daughters out to get on the bus for the first day of school. They were insistent that I take out my phone and film a video of them before the bus arrived.

I had no idea what they wanted, but I complied with their wishes anyway. The completely unsolicited message they subsequently delivered in the video melted my heart.

In unison, they said, "First day of school, and we're going to be good teammates this year."

What has become my life's mission all started with a simple attempt to instill the idea of being a good teammate in the hearts and minds of my daughters. When I heard what they said, my eyes welled up with tears.

Yesterday, my daughters boarded the bus for the final day of the school year. I wasn't able to be out at the bus stop with them, so you can imagine my reaction when my wife texted me the—once again—*unsolicited* video they demanded she film before they got on the bus.

"Last day of school, and we were good teammates this year."

I don't know if what they said is entirely true. I don't know if they were always good teammates this year. But I know their words are a clear indication that the seed I planted in them is taking root and growing more every day. They are cognizant of what it means to be a good teammate and that it is important to be one in life.

That seed isn't taking root just from my efforts. It's also being nurtured by the modeling and encouragement provided by their school teachers, who are affirming daily what it truly means to be a good teammate.

So I offer a heartfelt thank you to all of the great teachers who were good teammates this year. Your efforts were not in vain.

As always, remember: Good teammates care. Good teammates share. Good teammates listen. Go be a good teammate.

The Never-Ending Dance of the Good Teammate
JUNE 13

Isn't it funny how sometimes the normal everyday experiences of our life lead to the most insightful realizations?

This past weekend I had the pleasure of attending my daughters' dance recital. I don't know very much about dance, and I certainly don't have the skills needed to ever be a dancer, but what I do have is a genuine appreciation for talent. And I saw a lot of it at that dance show.

I have pointed out on previous occasions that it doesn't take talent to be a good teammate, but being a good teammate is a talent.

While I was watching the dance recital, it occurred to me how closely the talent of a good teammate resembles the talent of a good dancer. I would even take it a step farther and say that the *art* of being a good teammate is like a never-ending dance.

In this instance, I am not focusing on the dancer's talent in terms of things like hard work, dedication, determination, etc.

Those are omnipresent in the development of all types of talent. I'm not referring to flexibility or agility, or skills like that either.

The specific element of dance talent that caught my attention involves timing and spacing.

When dancers are doing solo performances, it is hard to tell when they make timing or spacing mistakes. If they start a move a beat too soon or too late, you don't really know if it was supposed to be that way, or not. The same thing is true if they make a move on center stage instead of stage left. You just cannot tell if it is a mistake or just bad choreography.

It is slightly easier to spot timing and spacing mistakes with a duo, but it can still be a challenge.

When a third dancer is added to the performance, however, it becomes obvious when the spacing and/or timing is off. The third dancer becomes a reference point.

If one dancer does a pirouette before the other two, you may not know if she was too early or if the other two were too late, but you definitely know something was off in the performance. That's timing.

If the dancers are in a line on stage, and there is a nine-foot gap between the middle and left dancers, but only a six-foot gap between the middle and right dancers, you know someone is not in the correct position. That's spacing.

My daughters were some of the recital's youngest performers. One of the dances they were involved in was a three-person dance to Twisted Sister's song "We're Not Gonna Take It." The theme of the dance was *girl power*, with the dancers' costumes fashioned to resemble success female professionals—a businesswoman, a doctor, and a policewoman.

Even at their age, I could spot the skill displayed in terms of adjusting their spacing on stage.

When one girl was nine feet away from the middle dancer, either the middle girl or the third girl had to adjust their spacing on the fly to accommodate the first dancer's spacing. It didn't really matter if the gap was choreographed to be six feet, or seven feet, or whatever, the fact was she was spaced at nine feet and the other dancers had to make an adjustment to cover her misstep.

They couldn't control her spacing, they could only control and adjust their own spacing.

The real challenge is that during the performance, they couldn't point out the mistake in spacing to the other dancer. It's not like they could just yell for her to move forward. Maybe the instructor could do that during the rehearsals, but not during the live performance. As the saying goes, the show must go on. And as it does, you must learn to be poised and professional.

The same is true for being a good teammate. You cannot control the "spacing" (*attitudes, actions, choices, etc.*) of your teammates. You can only control how you act and react.

Just like a dancer, you must constantly adjust to accommodate the missteps of your fellow teammates— counter and balance movements. It's that constant willingness to make adjustments for the betterment of the team that ultimately defines the kind of teammate you are.

As the line in the John Michael Montgomery country song goes, "Life's a dance you learn as you go. Sometimes you lead. Sometimes you follow." That line captures the essence of the never-ending dance that is the art of being a good teammate.

As always, remember: Good teammates care. Good teammates share. Good teammates listen. Go be a good teammate.

When Good Teammates Grow Up to Be Good Fathers
JUNE 20

Teammate Tuesdays have become a welcomed time of reflection for me. In many ways, they have evolved into an opportunity to just pause and take a look back at the week that was—to take stock on where I am in life and where I aspire to go. Based on the feedback I get from readers, I am not the only one who has this experience.

Last weekend, Americans celebrated Father's Day, and that holiday was the stimulus for my most recent round of reflections.

I love being a dad. I love EVERY single aspect of being a dad.

We spent Father's Day this year at a family gathering at my wife's grandfather's home. He is a wonderful father and a fascinating man.

Not long ago, the World War II veteran celebrated his 90th birthday, and to commemorate the occasion he wrote a book called "Battle Tested: Street kid. Soldier. Teacher. Patriarch."

It is the story of his life and a true testament to the values and grit that earned his contemporaries the title of "The Greatest Generation."

I could easily write this entire piece about him and the numerous attributes of his generation, but what I would like to focus on is what I observed while sitting around the gathering, watching the interactions of the other family members.

It was very clear to me that I was surrounded by good fathers. Everywhere I looked, I saw another good father. Uncles, cousins, nephews…they were ALL good fathers.

Instead of going golfing, or lounging around, or engaging in some other self-indulging activity—all of which are generally considered socially acceptable choices for dads on Father's Day—these men were actively playing with their children and grandchildren.

They wanted to spend time with their kids. They wanted to give their kids attention. They wanted to serve their kids' needs. That is how they *wanted* to spend Father's Day.

These men were not just good fathers, they were good teammates.

Good teammates want to be around their team. They want to serve the needs of the team, and have little interest in self-indulging activities. It is never about them. It is always about the team.

Good fathers are good teammates, because they prioritize their family—their team.

I have to believe there is a ripple effect to being a good father. For my wife's side of the family, the ripple effect certainly started with their patriarch, her grandfather.

His commitment to his family was modeled and copied from one generation to the next generation. And it continues to spread and affect his extended family.

When I got home that evening, I saw photos some of my former players had posted on social media of how they spent their Father's Day.

Those photos made my heart smile.

I loved looking at them because I loved seeing the kind of fathers they turned out to be.

(Sometimes the hardest part of coaching is the 10-15 year deferment to see if the most important lessons you tried to teach and emphasize to your players took root.)

The interesting thing about the ripple effect is eventually those ripples meet the shoreline, or a wall of some sort, and start to reverberate back towards the origin.

For me, those reverberations come in the form of me being inspired by those players and learning from them what it means to be a good father. Indeed, good teammates grow up to be good fathers.

A tip of the hat to all fathers who are also good teammates.

As always, remember: Good teammates care. Good teammates share. Good teammates listen. Go be a good teammate.

Nana's Band
JUNE 27

Almost 20 years ago, I was a counselor at a youth camp in Europe when I rounded a corner in the hallway and quite literally bumped into a lady who was trying to register her grandchildren for the camp.

That chance encounter was the beginning, as the saying goes, of a beautiful friendship.

Her grandson grew up to become one of my dearest friends. In fact, he became more than a friend, he became family—and so did his grandmother.

"Nana" is a fascinating lady. She has pizazz and an unmatched level of energy. As if that weren't enough, she is one of the kindest persons I've ever met.

Recently, we gathered to celebrate her 83rd birthday. It was an incredibly fun day, and a genuine celebration of her life.

During the party, she showed me two interesting photos. One made me laugh, the other made my jaw drop.

The first photo was a shot of me and her grandson taken the week he attended that youth camp all those years ago. It made me laugh, because it was taken during my pre-*follically*

29

challenged days, and I was reminded of how much hair I used to have. (In hindsight, maybe tears should have been the more appropriate emotional response, instead of laughter!)

The second photo was taken at a party Nana's family had thrown for her father on his 65th birthday. The picture captured a much younger version of Nana on the dance floor with her father. It is a touching moment that happened to be captured on film.

What made my jaw drop, though, was the band Nana pointed out to me in the background of the photo.

Nana is from Liverpool, England and her family had hired a local band to play at her father's party.

Diehard Fab Four fans can already guess where this story is going. For everyone else, the band in the background is the foundation of Rock and Roll legends, the Beatles.

Yes, it was a very young Liverpudlian by the name of John Lennon behind the microphone, with Paul McCartney and George Harrison performing alongside him.

So…what does this photo have to do with being a good teammate? Not a lot, really.

I just found Nana's photo to be fascinating and wanted to share—because that is what good teammates do, they share.

The more I thought about the photo, the more I started wondering about how many times I may have snapped a picture and some yet-to-be-famous person happened to be in the background.

When I got back home, I went on a mission to try and unearth one of those rare photos that I had perhaps taken.

I thought surely that type of thing must happen all the time, especially in the era of selfies and readily available camera phones.

Sadly, I didn't come across any such photos.

But as I rummaged through my photo albums, I did derive a sense of pleasure from looking at my old team photos.

I was reminded of how many good teammates I played with and coached over the years, and how often—like Nana's Beatles photo—those individuals somehow seemed to get lost in the background.

The reality is that what made being a part of those teams so enjoyable for me was the good teammates on them.

Find some time today to peruse your old photos and take a moment to reflect on how grateful you are to have had your special teammates by your side.

And if you happen to stumble upon any photos that may have an undiscovered celebrity in the background, make sure you *share* them with me.

As always, remember: Good teammates care. Good teammates share. Good teammates listen. Go be a good teammate.

Independence Day for Teammates
JULY 4

Today, Americans celebrate the Fourth of July—Independence Day. Since a fair amount of the subscribers to my blog are actually British, I would prefer not to focus this edition of *Teammate Tuesday* on the reason for the holiday, but instead on the topic of independence.

The idea of being a good teammate ultimately comes down to making decisions based on what is best for your team.

Quite often, this means having the self-discipline to suppress your natural desire for personal independence.

Recently, I was on a trip that required several vehicles to travel convoy-style to our destination. None of us were familiar with the area, so we relied on GPS to guide us. (That's *sat-nav* for our British readers.)

We each had GPS in our respective vehicles, and could have each gone our separate ways and met up at our final destination. But what if one of us had a flat tire or broke down? The wisest decision seemed for us to stay together.

Traveling in a convoy is a fascinating exercise in teamwork.

The driver in front—the de facto leader—has a lot of decisions to make that will impact the entire convoy (*the team*).

You must pick the right speed. If you go too slow, you endanger the safety of everyone in the convoy. If you go too fast, you not only put yourself at risk for getting a speeding ticket, but you put the entire group at risk.

And it is a risk that is multiplied by every vehicle in the convoy. If any of the vehicles gets pulled over it would lead to a substantial delay in travel time for everyone.

You must also consider the ramifications for the convoy each time you make a lane change or go through a traffic light.

Can the whole convoy make it through that yellow light before it turns red? Maybe you can make it through just fine, but can the *entire* group make it through? If not, your decision will break up the convoy. The same logic applies to changing lanes.

For the second vehicle in the convoy, and all subsequent vehicles, traveling this way becomes an experiment in the art of being a good follower.

In many ways, it is simply a matter of keeping up. But...anyone who has ever been in this situation knows it can be a lot harder than it sounds.

You have to really focus on the driver in front of you and keep pace. If you don't keep pace with that driver, other cars will get in between you and break up the convoy.

You have to anticipate lane changes and time them so they coincide with the lead vehicle. Delays in doing so could prevent you from moving over and would eventually also break up the convoy.

All of that is hard enough, but the real challenge comes in the form of suppressing your natural tendency to do these things from within your own comfort zone.

For instance, maybe you're the type of driver who likes to take it easy and observe the surrounding scenery as you cruise along the highway. You can't do it under these circumstances. You need to be attentive to the lead vehicle or you'll inevitably miss a lane change and lose the convoy.

Or, maybe you're the type of driver who likes to get from point A to point B as fast as possible and generally considers speed limits to be a mild suggestion. You can't do it under these circumstances, either. You need to get beyond your natural preference for expedience and get in sync with the pace of the rest of the group.

Obviously, the exact opposite scenario is also true. Perhaps you're the type of driver who never breaks the speed limit. You may find the lead driver keeping up with traffic and exceeding the posted speed limit.

For the betterment of the convoy, you will need to get beyond your natural comfort zone, assume the risk, and travel at the higher speed.

Sometimes, jointly assuming the added risk is what it means to be functioning as part of a team and not just and independent individual.

However, this raises an interesting question, how much risk is too much? At some point, shouldn't you consider the risk of traveling too fast in regard to the passengers in your own particular vehicle?

Let's not even look at speed, and the possible ethics of that issue. Let's instead look at something less controversial, like the potential issue of fuel. What happens if your vehicle gets low on fuel and you need to stop and refuel, but the other vehicles in the convoy do not.

You don't get a choice when it comes to fuel. If you run out, your vehicle doesn't go any farther. You *must* stop and refuel. Otherwise, there is no convoy for you.

This is where the concept of prioritizing your teams factors into the equation.

Maybe that prioritization comes in the form of you needing to stop and refuel your vehicle. Or maybe it comes in the form of you needing to take time off work to care of an elderly parent or a sick child.

If you communicate the urgency of your needs, the convoy will stop and allow you to refuel. Otherwise, it's not a *real* team and you have an obligation to the passengers in your vehicle to break free from the convoy and seek independence…metaphorically.

As always, remember: Good teammates care. Good teammates share. Good teammates listen. Go be a good teammate.

Darnell the Mover
JULY 11

Every so often, I encounter the most amazing teammates in the most unlikely places.

A few years ago, it was a busboy at a pizzeria in Cumberland, Maryland. Not long before that, it was a window washer in Spartanburg, South Carolina.

These individuals are genuine assets to their organizations—their teams. They somehow seem to move faster and get more done than everyone else. They also seem to have exceptionally positive attitudes and take a tremendous amount of pride in their work, no matter how insignificant that work may be perceived to be.

The busboy cleared his tables quicker and with more enthusiasm for busing tables than anyone I had ever seen. The wait time at his restaurant was greatly reduced because of how fast he got the tables ready. Customers were happy. Management was even more happy.

The window washer moved just as fast, yet had no tolerance for any streaks or missed spots on his glass.

They both took <u>PRIDE</u> in their craft. The actual craft was irrelevant to them, but the pride part mattered. You could see it in their eyes.

Recently, my family and I moved. And as anyone who has ever endured the process of moving will attest, it is not a particularly pleasant experience.

However, this moving experience proved to be otherwise, as I once again stumbled across one of those *amazing* teammates.

When the moving truck pulled up, I noticed only the driver got out of the vehicle. This concerned me.

I asked the driver if he had a crew coming to help, to which he nonchalantly replied, "No, just me and Darnell. He'll be here soon."

As the driver proceeded to make preparations for the unload, I took a look at the humungous tractor-trailer filled with our *stuff,* and thought to myself, "I hope this Darnell character is built like a Greek god, otherwise, this is going to take forever."

When Darnell finally arrived on the scene, I was disappointed to discover there was nothing Herculean about him.

In fact, the only thing relatively noteworthy about his physical stature was his uncanny resemblance to Will Smith's sidekick on the *Fresh Prince of Bel-Air*, DJ Jazzy Jeff. *(No offense intended to either party!)*

But as the saying goes, you shouldn't judge a book by its cover. Darnell soon reminded me of this.

I witnessed him lift the heaviest boxes and pieces of furniture with ease, time and time again. He had a technique where he sort of slung the boxes on his back and took off— with expedience.

It was impressive to watch him work. It was *more* impressive to listen to him work.

Darnell was a fountain of positivity. As he lugged another big box up the steps, he looked at my wife with his golden smile and said, "Do what you love. Love what you do. And I just love helping people."

While Darnell and the driver were unloading their truck, another delivery truck from a local company where we had bought some new pieces of furniture arrived at my house. They weren't supposed to arrive until later in the day.

The understandable reaction for the moving company would have been to complain about our lack of coordination and be angered by the inconvenience.

Darnell's response: "No problem. We just got to all play in the same sandbox. That's all. It'll be alright."

Most people don't respond that way. They want to assign blame and have things resolved for their benefit. They can't see beyond their own desires.

But Darnell's response is how good teammates think and react.

Good teammates think SHARE. They think about what is best for the team and not what is best for their immediate needs. In this case, Darnell understood my family didn't deliberately intend to inconvenience him. He also understood that working with the other delivery truck would keep us happy.

Happy customers mean referrals and repeat business for the moving company—his team.

Ironically, there was a moment when the men from the delivery company were struggling to figure out how to get an awkwardly-shaped piece of furniture up the stairs. Darnell stepped right in and helped them.

He didn't roll his eyes. He didn't stop to complain. He took action and helped them.

Afterwards, I asked Darnell how he came to have such a positive attitude. "You got to realize, life is short and you only get one time around. You can't just get on a treadmill and zombie out," he replied.

His response made my heart smile.

He went on to tell me that he has been married for 26 years and is the proud father of three daughters. That means he understands loyalty too.

I have become increasingly more aware lately of how valuable enthusiastic, positive-minded individuals like Darnell are to successful organizations.

Without them, progress is begrudgingly achieved…if achieved at all. Teammates with attitudes and energy like Darnell allow the team's success to flow freely.

When the move was complete and Darnell headed out the door for the final time, I heard him say, to no one in particular, "Peace and tranquility. Wow! What a beautiful day today is."

Darnell, thank you for making our moving experience one to remember and for reminding us all of the significant impact one good teammate can have on even the most dreaded endeavor.

I hope Darnell's company appreciates what an asset he is to them.

As always, remember: Good teammates care. Good teammates share. Good teammates listen. Go be a good teammate.

Five Ways to Show Interest
JULY18

A guilty pleasure I happen to enjoy to the fullest is *people watching*. I genuinely like sitting in public places and just observing people interact with one another.

For me, it is an opportunity to appreciate that good people come in all shapes and sizes. Ethnicity, geography, culture, fashion, etc. are all relative when you zero in on the interactions.

Recently, I was waiting for a table at a restaurant, engaged in another round of people watching, when I happened to overhear a woman talking about a meeting she had earlier that day with her supervisor. *(Yes, sometimes people watching leads to eavesdropping. But they are strangers to me, so I feel comfortable filing my poor manners under the heading "no harm, no foul.")*

It had apparently been a very positive meeting for this woman, as evidenced by her facial expressions and enthusiastic tone. What really caught my attention, though, was that she kept repeating the phrase, "I am just so grateful he took an interest in me."

I knew exactly what she was feeling.

Having someone take an interest in you is such a powerful experience. You feel bonded to them in a unique way. You find yourself wanting to please them, and going out of your way to not let them down.

If you have ever had a favorite teacher, coach, or boss, you understand.

From a teammate perspective, taking an interest in a fellow teammate is actually one of the keys to being a good teammate.

Doing so is a relatively easy endeavor and can be accomplished with minimal effort. However, conveying your interest can sometimes be challenging.

With that in mind, here are five simple ways to convey interest in a teammate:

1. LEAN FORWARD

Body language matters. In fact, sociologists consistently point out that body language accounts for more than half of all communication, and leaning forward is the most likely posture to convey interest. When a teammate is speaking to you, and you lean forward, you let him or her know you are receptive, if not eager, to hear what is being said.

2. NOD YOUR HEAD

As your teammate is speaking, nod your head. This gesture doesn't necessarily send the message that you are agreeing with what is being said, as much as it lets the speaker know you are listening and trying to process the message. The real value to nodding your head, however, is in the encouragement it gives the speaker to keep going. By simply nodding your head, you can encourage teammates to go further and share deeper thoughts than they otherwise would have. I know from personal experience, whenever I am speaking to an audience and I notice someone in the crowd nodding their head, I feel like I am making a connection and grow increasingly inspired.

3. ASK QUESTIONS

What reinforces interest more than curiosity? Not much. When you ask follow up questions, you let your teammates know you heard what they said…and you want to know more. Of course, no question does this better than *Why?* Allowing a teammate to answer *Why?* questions can empower them to feel like an expert and give you an insightful glimpse into their psyche.

4. OFFER SUMMATIONS

Whenever your teammates pause to take a breath, reiterate back to them what they just said to you. In keeping with the previous point of asking questions, you can even phrase your summation in the form of a question and achieve the same result. For example:

> *Speaker:* "I have never worn the red shirt."
> *You:* "So, you've never worn the red shirt?"

Summations let the speaker know you are listening and reassure him or her that it is OK to divulge more.

5. REVISIT

Allow some time to pass—maybe a few hours or even a few days—and then circle back to the topic of your previous conversation. If your teammate talked to you about a problem they were having with another teammate, ask how things are working out and if they are getting any better. If the topic of your conversation was dog grooming, print off an article you came across about tips for selecting a new dog groomer and share it with your teammate. A small gesture like that can pay big dividends and go a long way towards making you a better teammate.

As always, remember: Good teammates care. Good teammates share. Good teammates listen. Go be a good teammate.

When Your Demons Are Holding You
JULY 25

I am struggling to let go of a post that recently appeared on my personal Facebook timeline. It was a photo accompanied by the caption: "It's hard to let go of the demons inside; they were holding you when no one else would."

Normally, I would just shake my head and scroll down after reading something on social media to which I didn't necessarily agree. However, I felt obliged to comment this time.

My reply to this post was very simply:

"I disagree. You are stronger than ANY demon you think you have. And they were never holding you, they were just holding you back and distracting you from the ones who really love you."

It's been several days since I replied, but I still can't seem to let it go.

I did a little research, and although I was unable to pinpoint the exact origin of the quote, I did discover that photo is quite popular in certain circles and has been around for a while. This was just the first time it happened to appear on my timeline.

I suppose I originally replied because I care about the individual who made the post. I don't consider him to just be a Facebook friend, I consider him to be a teammate. I wanted him to know that people care about him and his wellbeing, and I felt *that* message needed to be shared with him.

This is what teammates do. They care. They share. And they listen. My reply was meant to be a sign to him that I was listening.

Since replying, though, my words have had some time to marinate in my mind and I have been thinking a lot about how difficult it can be to let go of our demons—those habits that are detrimental to us becoming the best version of ourselves.

Metaphorical demons can come in all shapes and sizes. It's easy to see the comforting effect they *seem* to have on our lives, especially during turbulent, stressful times. Our demons can indeed emerge to be a place of retreat, and even escape. They become the crutch that we are fooled into believing is holding us steady.

But…they aren't holding us steady. They are holding us back.

Not long ago I spoke at an event in a community that is being ravished by the opioid epidemic. I respect how challenging it can be to defeat a substance abuse addiction, and speaking to that audience gave me an even greater appreciation for that challenge.

I don't purport to fully understand the intricacies of treating an addiction, but I do believe that prevention often lies in getting individuals to not see themselves as individuals, but rather as members of a team.

When individuals see themselves this way, they start to consider the ramifications of their actions on those around them—their teammates. In that moment before they allow their demons to take hold, they don't think about themselves. They instead think about their teammates, and they make their choices based on what is best for their team.

The irony is that when individuals choose to serve the needs of their team, they find purpose in their own life. Purpose leads to fulfillment, which leads to happiness—a place void of demons.

While some demons are certainly more serious than others, all of them have the potential to negatively impact our team and prevent us from being good teammates.

Your demon might not involve substance abuse. Your demon might be the amount of time you're spending on your cell phone, or the lack of affection you're extending towards your spouse.

Whatever the case may be, decide today to find a way to stop letting your demons hold you back from being a better teammate. Letting go is the key to moving forward.

As always, remember: Good teammates care. Good teammates share. Good teammates listen. Go be a good teammate.

Victory Cake
AUGUST 1

If you spend any amount of time on social media, you've at some point surely had the thought that "Every day is something day!"

National Talk Like A Pirate Day. National Underwear Day. National Skip Rope Day. National Sneak Some Zucchini Into Your Neighbor's Porch Day. (Yes, that is a real thing!)

I shake my head and chuckle at most of the designations. But every now and then, one pops up to which I don't particularly mind partaking. This past weekend was one of those occasions.

It was National Cheesecake Day.

I happen to really like cheesecake. However, that is not the main reason I was excited to celebrate that *holiday*.

In my house, we call cheesecake "Victory Cake." There is of course a story behind the distinction.

Years ago, I crossed paths with an older, wiser basketball coach who relayed to me how important it is to *celebrate your victories*—to make a deliberate effort to pause and enjoy the post-win moment before moving onto the next event.

How you celebrate, isn't nearly as important as why you celebrate.

Winning is not easy. Achievement in general is not easy. It typically does not happen without sacrifice and significant effort. And…usually a little luck. By celebrating your victory, you are not just rewarding yourself, you're paying homage to the sacrifices made.

As a coach, celebrating victories came in the form of me indulging in the guilty pleasure of eating cheesecake. Whenever my team won a game, I made it a point to stop on the way home from the game for a slice of cheesecake.

After a team victory eventually became the only occasion when I would eat cheesecake.

I never spoke of this personal, unwritten policy to my family, but that didn't mean it went unnoticed.

One day, out of the blue, my four-year old said to me: "Daddy, can I have a piece of that victory cake?"

I knew exactly what she was talking about.

I may not have ever mentioned it to her, but she had been watching and took note that her father always ate cheesecake after his team won.

And so, the term "Victory Cake" was coined.

Over the years, our family has used cheesecake to celebrate more than just wins on the court. If my wife gets a promotion at work, we eat cheesecake. If my daughter aces her spelling test in school, we eat cheesecake. If her younger sister loses a tooth, forget about the Tooth Fairy, it's time for victory cake. (Sometimes, victories are relative to the celebrant!)

Celebrate your victories has proven to be some of the best advice I was ever given. It has become a life-theme for our family. It is something we take very seriously.

There was a time, though, when I was fearful that celebrating my victories would be perceived as bragging. I was afraid someone might think I was trying to rub my good fortune in their face.

But I no longer feel that way.

Victory cake has bonded my family—my team. It has allowed us to share in the enjoyment of each other's accomplishments and to appreciate that when one of us wins, we all win.

Being able to rejoice in another's accomplishment is a hallmark of a good teammate.

An individual who has jealousy in their heart can never really be a good teammate. If someone is jealous of your victory, then they aren't a real teammate to you, and you shouldn't waste your time worrying about them.

Furthermore, when you celebrate your victories and share the occasion, you inspire others.

Sharing is also a hallmark of a good teammate.

With that in mind, I am going to type these last few keystrokes and then head out for a piece of victory cake to celebrate the completion of another *Teammate Tuesday* blog.

I hope you'll find a way to celebrate the victories in your life today, too.

As always, remember: Good teammates care. Good teammates share. Good teammates listen. Go be a good teammate.

*(*By the way, in case you were still wondering, National "Sneak Some Zucchini Into Your Neighbor's Porch Day" is on August 8.)*

When the Family Is a Team
AUGUST 8

So often in sports we hear coaches try to compare their team to a family. It is intended to be a very positive and encouraging assessment. However, it is also a cliché that I'm not always sure translates to all young athletes.

The reason is because some players grow up in broken homes with dysfunctional families, and don't necessarily understand what a healthy family is, nor how one operates.

For those athletes, being asked to be a part of a team that functions like a family isn't a particularly appealing invitation.

The flipside of that scenario happens to also be true.

Last week, I traveled to West Virginia to speak to a group of Title I parents. It was a wonderful group and I really enjoyed spending time with them.

The topic of my presentation was *Seeing Your Family as a Team.*

Just as players who lack familiarity with a healthy family model struggle to understand teams functioning like families, there are families who are not well-versed in sports and find it difficult to understand the concept of a team.

As I always do, I pointed out to the audience that every organization strives to incorporate the concept of teamwork into their operations. But the reality is that teamwork will never happen without the infusion of good teammates— individuals who have a "team-first" mindset and a willingness to make sacrifices for their team.

I also explained to them the three elements that differentiate a team from just another group. I would like to now share this information with you (...*because good teammates share!*):

1. TEAMS HAVE COMMONALITY

Sometimes the easiest way to notice commonality is in the team's uniformity. The Pittsburgh Steelers all wear black and gold. The New York Yankees all wear pinstripes.

Although I have met plenty of families who love their camouflage and do seem to arguably have a family "uniform," families don't have to dress alike to have commonality. It can come in the form of a shared fondness for Disney or a particular television show. Commonality can be achieved by simply living under the same roof or traveling together in the same vehicle.

2. TEAMS HAVE DEFINED ROLES

Quarterbacks pass. Running backs run. Linemen block. Linebackers tackle. Every position on a football team has a role. Likewise, parents are parents and children are supposed to be children. Each of those roles is accompanied by its own unique set of responsibilities.

When who does what role gets muddied, dysfunction inevitably occurs. When the behavior of the parent forces the child to take on the role of being the responsible adult in the family, it is the same as a lineman deciding to become the player who passes the ball instead of the player who is supposed to be blocking.

Everybody has a role, and everybody does their role to the best of their ability.

3. TEAMS HAVE A SHARED OBJECTIVE

The Pittsburgh Steelers are trying to win the Super Bowl. The New York Yankees are trying to win the World Series.

What is the objective of your family? Do you have one? The best families do.

In my family, we want to use the gifts we were given to help others and make the world a better place. That is our family objective, and it remains at the forefront of our daily choices.

If you can get your family to have commonality, defined roles, and shared objectives, then you can get your family to be more than a group. You can get them to be a team—a winning team.

As always, remember: Good teammates care. Good teammates share. Good teammates listen. Go be a good teammate.

First Day of School
AUGUST 15

It's that time of year again. Back to school. With the abundance of store specials and advertisements on television, the occasion has practically achieved holiday status.

One of the most heartwarming moments of my life came on the morning of the first day of school last year.

As we stood near the end of my driveway, anxiously waiting the school bus's arrival, my daughters turned to me and asked me to take my phone out and film a video.

I wasn't initially inclined to acknowledge their request, but they were persistent.

"Daddy, please...PLEASE...use your phone to film this video!"

Eventually, I caved in to their demands. And I am glad I did, because what transpired next has had a substantial impact on my life.

Sporting big smiles and with their arms locked around each other's necks, my daughters looked into the lens and very eloquently said, "First day of school, and we're going to be good teammates this year."

Their impromptu—and unsolicited—proclamation, put a lump in my throat. Of all the possible words they could have spoken, I did not expect to hear those words.

My interest in the *good teammate mindset* developed from a desire to offer a bit of final advice to my daughters if something should ever happen that would preclude me from being in their lives.

That desire is what led to my children's book *Be A Good Teammate*.

My daughters' choice in words that morning meant so much to me because they provided validation to my efforts.

I planted a seed in their hearts and had put considerable effort into nurturing that seed and trying to get it to take root.

As any parent, teacher, or coach will attest, it can be incredibly frustrating to figure out if the lesson taught is being absorbed.

The message from my daughters' video assured me that the lesson was in fact being absorbed. That video inspired me to dive deeper into the subject of being a good teammate and put more effort into sharing what I've discovered with others.

Yesterday, my daughters embarked on the start of another school year. Once again, they asked me to film a video of them before they left for school. I had a clue what the subject of the video might be this time, so I wasn't quite as surprised.

However, my daughters were attending a new school this year and I was nervous about the transition.

Enrolling in a new school can be an incredibly stressful situation for any kid. In this case, and judging by the tone of their most recent video, I suspect I was stressing more about it than either of them were.

By relentlessly encouraging them to be good teammates, and reinforcing exactly what that means, I would like to believe that I gave them the confidence to handle the stress of this potentially traumatic experience.

The seed I planted was indeed taking root.

I had repeatedly told them that good teammates will always have friends because people of all ages have an inherent desire to be around individuals who care and who are kind.

When my daughters got home from school yesterday, I asked them the same three questions that I always do. *(Every parent knows it is like pulling teeth to get information out of their children when it comes to how the day went, so we've agreed to allow me three guaranteed questions every day after school.)*

> *Question 1:* What did you eat for lunch today?
>
> *Question 2:* Who did you play with at recess today?
>
> *Question 3:* Did you make any *good teammates moves* today?

The first two questions are just set-up questions, although I am usually humored by their answers. What I really want, though, is to hear the answers to the third question.

Good teammate moves are all of those little gestures of kindness that may be minor inconveniences to us, but make all the difference in someone else's life.

It's sharing your crayons with a classmate that doesn't have any. It's helping a classmate pick up the papers that scattered from the folder they dropped. It's giving a classmate a hug when they are sad. It is standing up to a bully for your classmate.

I am never disappointed in the answers I get from my children. They always reaffirm the significance of teaching them to be good teammates.

If you have children, make an effort tonight to ask them if they made any *good teammate moves* today. In time, their answers will inspire you too.

When you're done with your children, take a look in the mirror and ask yourself the same question.

What *good teammate moves* did you make today?

The world cannot have too many good teammates…and it's never too late to become a better teammate.

As always, remember: Good teammates care. Good teammates share. Good teammates listen. Go be a good teammate.

That Kid Jake
AUGUST 22

I am writing this week's blog with a very heavy heart.

Early in my coaching career, I was assigned the task of coaching my institution's men's soccer team. As a basketball coach, I knew very little about the sport of soccer. But it was common practice at that time for coaches at the small college level to have to coach more than one sport, so I begrudgingly accepted the assignment.

We had six students show up at our first practice—obviously, insufficient number to field a team.

That meant that job #1 was to find enough bodies to meet our required roster.

I started to ask the players who did show up for the first practice if they knew of any other students who may consider joining us. They brainstormed for several minutes, when I heard one of them say, "What about that kid Jake?"

That kid Jake.

I am not sure why, but there was something about the tone of his question that piqued my interest.

That kid Jake.

Turns out Jake, who was arguably too old to still be referred to as a kid, was a former Division I football player, who changed majors and recently transferred to our school.

His previous school had a football team, but didn't offer his major. We offered his major, but didn't have a football team.

I wondered if he would consider a change of sports, so I set out to find *that kid Jake*.

I scoured the campus for the next few hours, until I eventually found Jake and two of his friends from high school hanging out in the student union.

When I approached him, he was initially reluctant to accept my proposal. He told me he never played soccer before and didn't know anything about the sport.

However, he seemed intrigued—if not humored—when I confided in him that neither did I.

A subsequent appeal to his competitive side tipped the scales in my favor. *That kid Jake* was onboard.

He showed up at our next practice, bringing with him his two friends from high school—who incidentally turned out to be brothers.

What the three of them lacked in soccer skills, they more than made up for in natural athleticism and competitiveness.

Jake became the team's goalkeeper. And although we gave up a lot of goals that season, and we didn't win any games, that group of students became one of my all-time favorite teams.

The assignment I so begrudgingly accepted turned out to be a tremendous blessing.

A big reason for me enjoying being around that team so much was *that kid Jake*.

He was the ultimate good teammate. He was consistently punctual, dependable, loyal, hard-working, etc. I don't think he ever had a single individualistic thought. It was always team-first for him.

He also had an infectious personality, and I certainly wasn't the only one who enjoyed being around him.

I had lost track of Jake over the years.

Last week, a photo of him came across my desk. Unfortunately, the photo was accompanied by sad news.

At a much too young age, Jake unexpectedly passed away.

The photo came via a mutual friend, and was a shot of Jake coaching her son's youth soccer team. My heart smiled when I learned that Jake became a soccer coach.

The friend who shared the photo with me raved about what a great coach he was, and how much her son adored him.

As I read Jake's obituary and the many online tributes that followed, it was evident to me that he successfully carried with him those same characteristics that made him a good teammate on the soccer field into his adult life.

He was a beloved husband, father, co-worker, and community leader.

What more could any coach ever hope for than to have that be the case with a former player?

In fact, striving to make that happen should be the primary goal of every sports coach.

He leaves behind a wife and three beautiful daughters.

A *GoFundMe* memorial account has been set up to help his family defray the costs of their loss.

If you have ever had the honor of having a good teammate like *that kid Jake*, I hope you will find it in your heart to make a good teammate move of your own and contribute to his memorial fund.

(https://www.gofundme.com/jacob-jake-ebersole-memorial-fund)

Rest in peace Jake...and know that your story was an inspiration to many others.

As always, remember: Good teammates care. Good teammates share. Good teammates listen. Go be a good teammate.

When You Represent More than Yourself
AUGUST 29

The fall sports season is upon us!

It's sad to see the summer come to an end, but it is exciting to see athletes of all ages return to the fields and courts for the beginning of their fall seasons.

To commemorate their return, I tweeted a bit of general advice to the fall athletes last Friday:

If you're taking the field/court tonight, remember: Good teammates understand they represent more than just themselves. #CLASS

Our *Be a Good Teammate* efforts hit a bit of a social media milestone recently when we passed the 10,000 followers mark on Twitter. We got a "K" added to our page!!! *(*That's how Twitter signifies 10,000...10K!)*

The movement is growing more every day, and it certainly makes my heart smile to know that others are buying in to the message and sharing it with members of their respective teams.

While my advice about players understanding they represent more than themselves was intended for the fall sports consortium, it is advice that is applicable to anyone who is on a team. And...*everybody* is on a team in some capacity.

Good teammates sincerely grasp the concept of representing something more than just themselves. They appreciate that the choices they make and the actions they take are a reflection of their team.

How that individual conducts himself or herself on the metaphorical playing field allows others to form opinions about the entire team. Good teammates always want their team to be cast in the best possible light.

Any unethical or unsportsmanlike conduct tarnishes the perception of their team. And since we usually belong to a lot of different teams (*our community, our organization, our family, etc.*), the images of more than just the immediate members of our team can also be tarnished by our poor choices.

The best teammates are not just aware of the situation, they consciously consider the ramifications of their choices before they act. They factor in the effect their choice will have on the perception of their team and then make their decision accordingly.

As the hashtag alludes, it's called class.

Good teammates have class.

On that note, I would like to take a moment to thank every one of those 10K followers for joining the *Be a Good Teammate* movement. Of course, I also extend my gratitude to everyone who follows along on Facebook and subscribes to this blog too. You are all good teammates, and together we are going to make *Team World* a better place.

As always, remember: Good teammates care. Good teammates share. Good teammates listen. Go be a good teammate.

Don't Feed the Gators
SEPTEMBER 5

If you spend any length of time in Florida, you will inevitably encounter an alligator. In fact, the occurrence is so common that warning signs are posted around communities with the intention of reducing the frequency of the encounters.

One of those such signs is posted by the lake in my community. It offers two very sound bits of advice:

1. *No swimming.*
2. *Do not feed alligators.*

If you spend any length of time on a team, you will inevitably encounter an alligator of your own—a toxic teammate. When you do, I recommend you heed the same advice that is on the aforementioned sign:

1. *No swimming.*
2. *Do not feed alligators.*

Obviously, swimming in alligator infested water, or any body of water that has even a single alligator in it for that matter, is a dangerous endeavor. You're putting yourself at risk for serious bodily harm by entering the water.

In regards to toxic teammates, *No swimming* means don't get involved with them. If you allow yourself to succumb to the same negativity, apathy, and malcontent as the toxic teammates, they will devour your enthusiasm and your team spirit with the same ferocity as an alligator attacking a swimmer.

Sometimes alligators can be hard to spot. They can hold their breath underwater for a considerable amount of time. In some cases, it can be as long as one hour. Even when they are not completely submerged, alligators typically expose only the very tip of their noses above the waterline.

Just because you don't see them right away, doesn't mean they are not in the water, lurking beneath the surface, waiting to attack. The same is true of toxic teammates.

The best way to avoid the attack is to not go in the water.

This brings us to the part about not feeding the alligators. When humans feed alligators, they tend to draw the alligators out of the water. In which case, it doesn't matter if you go swimming or not, the danger of the alligator will come to you.

Toxic teammates are constantly searching for sources of malcontent. As the saying goes, misery loves company.

When you do anything but disagree with a toxic teammate's dissatisfaction, you are in essence feeding their toxicity.

Just like the alligators, toxic teammates will grow increasingly bolder and less fearful, if they sense the availability of an easy source of food. That is why you cannot allow them to think you are anything but loyal to your team and its leadership.

There is an old wives' tale that says you can escape an alligator chasing you on land by running in a zig-zag pattern.

But it is just that—an old wives' tale. It's not really true.

Trying to escape the clutches of a toxic teammate by running in a zig-zag patter, i.e. gingerly dancing around the issue with noncommittal statements, doesn't work either. At best, it just temporarily stays off the toxicity.

Be definitive in your stance and make your loyalty to your team abundantly clear.

Alligators have very small brains. They don't play games and they are incapable of abstract thought. Their reptilian brain allows them to only think of meeting their primary individual needs, like eating.

Toxic teammates think the same way. They are capable of only seeing things in terms of what is best for them, not what is best for their team.

Good teammates don't swim with the gators on their team, and they don't feed them either, because they think in terms of what is best for the team.

As always, remember: Good teammates care. Good teammates share. Good teammates listen. Go be a good teammate.

Bend...But Don't Break
SEPTEMBER 12

Our family survived Hurricane Irma! As new Floridians, it was our first hurricane.

I wouldn't necessarily call that a commendable achievement, nor would I label it as a particularly fun experience. But I will say it was an experience that provided me with an even greater appreciation for the impact of good teammates.

In the wake of Hurricane Harvey, I tweeted a photo of Houston EMS personnel making good teammate moves by bravely aiding those in need. The photo was accompanied by the following text:

Photos coming out of Houston are incredible. Proof that good teammates always emerge in times of need. #HoustonStrong

When I tweeted that message, I didn't expect to be in the thralls of my own hurricane adventure a mere two weeks later.

Through the wonders of technology, I witnessed numerous acts of kindness with Harvey. With Irma, I got to witness them firsthand.

What I witnessed covered the gamut of selflessness. I saw everything from the tremendous courage of EMS personnel rescuing stranded victims to the seemingly small gestures of generosity between neighbors.

When Irma passed, a group of my neighbors went up and down our street securing and replanting every uprooted tree. No one asked them to do so. They just did it out of the kindness of their heart. Their gesture meant a lot to the residents of our community.

As first time *hurricaners*, it meant a lot to my family to have neighbors stop by and offer reassuring advice before Irma hit. Equally appreciated were the calls and texts we got checking in on us during the storm.

Although I was very grateful for those things, I don't know that I was particularly surprised by them. Catastrophic events always seem to bring out the best in people. It is one of life's great ironies.

What did surprise me, however, were the palm trees in front of my house.

I don't have much experience with palm trees. There aren't any of them where I grew up in western Pennsylvania.

I am not sure why, maybe it was their skinny appearance or my naivety, but I assumed the palm trees would be the first to snap when the winds reached hurricane levels. I was wrong.

Their branches thrashed in the wind, and their trunks swayed, but they didn't break.

We had other bigger, stronger trees in our neighborhood that didn't fare as well. When the storm was over, there were plenty of downed oak trees. But no palm trees.

We've all come across teammates who were like the oak trees. They are so rigid, and so headstrong, that they can't adapt. They are incapable of compromise. When they don't get their way, they abandon the needs of their team and resort to self-serving agendas. In essence, they break.

Good teammates are like palm trees. They bend, but they don't break.

They are able to bend their personal desires to match what's best for their team. They remain loyal without forsaking their integrity or abandoning their team. They bend, but they don't break.

We are blessed to be surrounded by such great friends and neighbors, and we were fortunate to have made it through Hurricane Irma as virtually unscathed as we did. I know many others were not as fortunate. And I know now is the time to step up and be good teammates to those individuals who weren't.

The sun is back shining today. It's almost hard to believe a hurricane just passed through.

If adversity is making its way through your team, choose to be a palm tree. Bend...but don't break. If you can weather the storm, the sun will eventually return to shining in your life too.

As always, remember: Good teammates care. Good teammates share. Good teammates listen. Go be a good teammate.

Making Good Teammate Moves
SEPTEMBER 19

When dancers hit the dance floor, they bust a move. And if they are a good dancer, they have good moves.

The same is true for athletes.

When basketball players hit the court, they make moves. They spin, shake, shuffle, crossover, etc. with the intention of scoring. If they are a good player, they will have good moves.

In fact, sometimes members of the media will even describe an especially good player as having "an arsenal of moves." Isn't that a vivid description of the potency of that player? An *arsenal* of moves.

My experience in studying good teammates has shown me that these individuals have an arsenal of moves of their own—a seemingly endless supply of selfless acts that benefit the other members of their team and their team as a whole. I have come to know these acts as *good teammate moves*.

If you walk down the hallway of your building and see a piece of trash, and then—without hesitation—proceed to pick up that trash and throw it in the trashcan, you are making a *good teammate move*.

You don't grumble about who threw it there, or whose job it is to pick it up, or how terrible it is that you had to be the one to pick it up. You just act.

If you walk through the parking lot at your grocery store and see a stray cart, and then—without hesitation—proceed to push that cart back into the store, you are making a good teammate move.

You don't grumble about who left it there, or whose job it is to push it back, or how terrible it is that you had to be the one to push it back. You just act.

You do these things because they are what's best for your team.

In the case of the loose shopping cart, you push it back into the store because the cart could cause damage if it rolls free and smashes into someone's car. Those "someones" live in your community and are your teammates. The citizens of successful communities act and see themselves as teammates.

Your small gesture of kindness—pushing the cart back into the store—benefited your community. You may have kept someone's car from being damaged. You may have helped the store keep its prices down. You may have reduced insurance premiums.

Interestingly, your action didn't really cost you anything extra at all, except maybe a little bit of time and effort. But it potentially made a big difference to your team.

This is a concept that I have tried to emphasize to my children. In a previous blog, I described how I ask my daughters the same three questions every day when they come home from school:

1. What did you eat for lunch today?
2. Who did you play with at recess today?
3. Did you make any *good teammate moves* today?

As any parent will attest, it is a challenge to get your children to provide details about their day. But asking them the same three question everyday seems to give them some routine in terms of what to expect when they get home. It also seems to have increased their willingness to disclose more information to me than I otherwise would have been able to obtain.

My first two questions are actually just set-up questions. They prime the communication pump, so to speak. I am more interested with their answers to the third question. *Did you make any good teammate moves today?*

I am consistently blown away by their answers. Some days it's hard to fight back tears of pride, because I am so touched by what they tell me.

Not long ago, my daughter told me the story of how she won a spelling contest and got to pick a prize form the treasure chest. She told me there is girl in her class who never has crayons of her own and always has to share the other kids' crayons. My daughter chose a box of crayons as her prize and then gave that box to the little girl who didn't have any of her own.

Good teammate move.

Another time, my daughter told me how she left her normal group of friends to go play with the new kid in her class on the playground.

Good teammate move.

Lately, my daughters have been packing an extra snack to take with them in the morning. At their school, the kids get a snack break every afternoon. Each student is supposed to bring their own snack. My daughters insist on packing an extra snack "just in case somebody in the class forgets theirs that day."

Who wouldn't want to be teammates with someone who thinks this way? How about friends, neighbors, or colleagues? I think everybody would.

It doesn't take any special talent to make *good teammate moves*.

You just need an open heart, a generous spirit, and a willingness to not mind being inconvenienced by going above and beyond. We are all capable of having those things. And we are all capable of being a good teammate.

All it takes is a simple shift in mindset.

What *good teammate moves* can you make today?

As always, remember: Good teammates care. Good teammates share. Good teammates listen. Go be a good teammate.

Respect Time
SEPTEMBER 26

If a sports team was getting ready to play an undefeated perennial powerhouse, you would expect to see a heightened level of focus in their preparation for that opponent.

They would bump up their effort because they have a greater respect for that opponent than most of their other opponents. Right or wrong, that's typically the way it is. Players know that a mediocre effort against an undefeated opponent will not yield a successful result. The situation demands their best.

As humans, we face a similar situation every day of our lives. The opponent? Time.

Time is undefeated. You cannot slow it down. You cannot derail it. And you certainly cannot stop it. It just keeps moving forward.

Time is U-N-D-E-F-E-A-T-E-D.

Good teammates understand this concept. They don't accept tardiness. In fact, many of them operate on "Lombardi Time" *(If you're 10 minutes early, you're 5 minutes late.)*

Sometimes we struggle to get our family out the door in the morning. I suspect most families with small children can relate to this.

Everybody has their own pace and their own priorities. Chaos ensues. And getting out the door on time becomes an exercise in futility.

The Loya household has recently adopted a phrase we speak to each other to help us refocus our efforts and curb the chaos: *RESPECT TIME.*

This is exactly what good teammates do. They respect time. They respect it the same way they respect an undefeated opponent.

Here are three ways you can respect time:

1. <u>PLAN</u>

Having a plan in place for how you intend to spend your time allows you to be more efficient and minimizes the amount of time you are likely to waste deciding what to do next.

I am a list maker. I like to make "To Do" lists before I go to bed at night. I separate my lists into two categories—standards and goals. Standards are all the things that I *need* to accomplish that day. This may include things like going to the bank, returning one of my client's calls, or going to a doctor's appointment.

If I fail to complete an item from my standards category, there are consequences. Sometimes those consequences can be severe.

Goals are things that I *want* to accomplish that day. Writing two chapters of my next book, cleaning out the garage, or reorganizing my files would fall under this heading.

If I fail to complete an item from the goals category, I just reevaluate it and decide if it should be added to the list again tomorrow. Incidentally, I used to compose my list before I went to bed at night so I could maximize my efficiency and hit the ground running the next morning. But that is not the only reason I do it this way anymore.

I have learned that letting something marinate overnight can lead me to rethink the necessity of that item and move it in the morning from the standards category to the goals category, or remove it from the list entirely.

2. PRACTICE AWARENESS

This is an increasingly important skill for a person to have. With so much evolving technology at our fingertips, it is easy to get lost in our own world and forget that the universe doesn't really revolve around the needs of our life.

I have friends who often suggest we go to the cinema to see a movie, but become frustrated to learn that the movie isn't playing at a time that is convenient for them.

Movie start times are already set. If you are heading out for an evening that includes a trip to the cinema, then you have to be aware of the start times and plan your other activities (dinner, shopping, drinks, etc.) around the start times.

I have another friend who struggles with being aware of how long it takes to do something. Driving from Point A to Point B takes 30 minutes. If your Point B meeting starts at 9:00 AM, you can't leave Point A at 8:40 AM and expect to be on time. You need to make an effort to be more aware of how much time is required for your daily tasks.

3. ADAPT AND/OR MANIPULATE

Similar to the previous point about awareness, you must be willing to alter your plans. For instance, if you need to be out the door at 9:00 AM, and it normally takes you an hour to get ready, then you need to start your routine at 8:00 AM.

However, if your alarm clock goes off late or an unexpected phone call causes you to not be able to start getting ready until 8:15 am, then you need to either adapt your normal routine or manipulate it.

You either change the pace at which you normally move through your routine, or you eliminate a component from it. Either way, 15 minutes must be made up, or you will be late.

The length of your shower might need to be shortened. The speed at which you walk down the hallway may no longer be able to be a leisurely stroll.

If you can't change the pace and condense, then you must eliminate something that you typically do during your routine.

You may not be able to have your normal relaxing cup of coffee before you get in the shower. Or, you may not even be able to get a shower.

It is surprising how many people are unable to make these kinds of alterations and consequently find themselves to be habitually at the mercy of time.

Good teammates respect time, because they respect honesty and trustworthiness. They would never steal. Showing up late for a team function, or even showing up unprepared, is stealing the team's most valuable possession—time.

As always, remember: Good teammates care. Good teammates share. Good teammates listen. Go be a good teammate.

The Happy Shirt Collection
OCTOBER 3

Look what I got in the mail this week!

A Hard Rock Café t-shirt from Aruba. I am a little taken back by it, to be honest. Let me explain...

I collect Hard Rock Café t-shirts. There is a wall in my house where the entire collection is prominently displayed. The story of how the collection got started is interesting in and of itself.

You see, a few decades ago, I was living overseas. One evening I was feeling particularly down and homesick.

I happened to be in London that evening, and as I walked the city's rainy streets I stumbled upon what I thought to be an American-themed restaurant. Dining in the confines of familiarity seemed like a good idea, so I went in and sat down.

Obviously, that establishment was the Hard Rock Café-London, and it did indeed turn out to be the perfect remedy for my blues.

As I sat at my table listening to the loud music and eating what I recall to be the most savory burger I had ever tasted, a warm feeling seemed to envelope me. My stress had dissipated. I was happy.

In fact, I felt so happy that I wanted to capture the essence of the moment. On my way out of the restaurant, I stopped in the gift shop and purchased a classic white Hard Rock Café t-shirt with the word London printed on the front. In doing so, I connected a good memory to a good emotion.

I loved that t-shirt. It quickly became my favorite article of clothing. I think I wore it everywhere I went because, at least subconsciously, I associated it with the feeling of happiness. That shirt became my *happy shirt.*

Over time, my London shirt started to become worn and frayed, as cotton t-shirts tend to do. One day, a few years later, I walked by a Hard Rock Café in Atlanta, so I stopped and had lunch…and bought another shirt. I subsequently did the same thing in Toronto. And in Pittsburgh. And in Washington, D.C.

Before I knew it, I had started a collection.

When the London shirt became so frayed that it was too fragile to wear anymore, I put it in a frame and hung it on the wall. My happy shirt became my happy picture.

I have acquired dozens of Hard Rock Café t-shirts since then. I don't even try to wear them anymore. I now put them straight into a frame and add them to the wall.

Having a collection of anything can be good for the soul. It can offer a visual cue to our past, a reminder of where we've been. It can also give us something to look forward to.

My Hard Rock Café collection certainly does that for me. I remember the details of obtaining each and every one of those t-shirts. My collection represents the adventures of my life and where my travels have taken me. Lots and lots of memories are captured in those framed shirts.

I enjoy looking forward to acquiring my next shirt and wonder what adventure will accompany that acquisition. My collection fuels my life's journey.

Which brings us to the Aruba shirt.

Last year, my wife celebrated a milestone birthday. *(I'll be a good teammate and not disclose which milestone it was!)* To celebrate the occasion, we took a trip to the Caribbean island of Aruba. Neither of us had been there before and we had heard wonderful things about the location.

In full disclosure, I may have had a "mild" ulterior motive in choosing Aruba, since it also had one of the few Hard Rock Cafes I had yet to visit.

When we ate dinner at the Hard Rock Café-Aruba, I was very disappointed to discover that the gift shop was out of stock of the white classic t-shirts I collected.

I explained my situation to the employee working the register, and she summoned the assistant manager. They apologized for the inconvenience and took my contact information with the promise to call me when they got the shirts back in stock.

When I returned home, I sent an email to the Hard Rock Café corporate office about the situation and my disappointment. The next day, I got a response from one of their customer service representatives.

Again, there was an apology for the inconvenience and they said they would have a member of the Aruba management contact me. Shortly after receiving that email, I did get an email from the general manager of the Hard Rock Café-Aruba.

The manager offered the same apology for the inconvenience and promised to make arrangements for me to purchase a t-shirt via email as soon as their shipment was delivered—even though this is against their normal policy.

Months passed, and I never heard from him or anyone else from the Hard Rock Café. I wrote it off as a life lesson and let it go.

I recently moved into a new house and had to re-hang my Hard Rock Café t-shirts. In the process of doing so, I grew annoyed that I was still missing the Aruba location—a blemish to my collection. I decided to send another email to the Hard Rock Café customer service department, after all, it had now been well over a year since they promised to contact me.

This time, the tone of my email was more reflective of my disappointment in the Hard Rock Café brand, and not just my inability to purchase a shirt.

I wrote:

"You didn't just fail to meet my expectations, you failed to uphold the standard of excellence that I have come to associate with the Hard Rock Cafe franchise."

I wrote that particular sentence with complete sincerely because I really believed it.

Within minutes of sending the email, I got a response from Fernando Davila, the Managing Director of the Hard Rock Café-Aruba, and from Giorgio Russo, the new General Manager. They again apologized and promised to get me a t-shirt ASAP.

Given what had previously transpired, my initial reaction to this promise was a very skeptical, "We'll see."

The next day, Esther, the Rock Shop Manager, requested my mailing address. A few days later, I got a courtesy call from Esther, just to let me know that Hurricane Maria was going to cause a slight delay in sending me the shirt, but to not fear because it would be going out in the mail as soon as possible.

You already know how the story ends.

So where is the good teammate lesson in all of this?

Good teammates are people of action. They go above and beyond to protect the image of the team, and they do so without hesitation. In this instance, my problem was handled the moment it got into the hands of a good teammate.

Fernando, Giorgio, and Esther were all good teammates. And I hope Hard Rock Café corporate realizes what assets they have in these individuals.

They embodied the three inalienable characteristics of all good teammates—care, share, and listen.

They listened to my problem, and they also viewed my problem as their team's problem.

They showed they cared about their corporate team, their company brand, and their customers by responding positively to me. And they shared their time and their energy to solve the problem,

They took a negative experience and turned it into a positive one. Their response built even more loyalty with me as a Hard Rock Café fan.

Customer service is a team within the team, and every team has its own version of a customer service department. It's those team members who are on the front lines, entrusted with the team's reputation. The best teams make sure their best teammates are put into those positions.

Those individuals are ultimately more than just ambassadors who control the team's image, they control the team's culture.

A very heartfelt thank you to the Hard Rock Café's customer service members for being good teammates and restoring my faith in their company—and the happiness I have come to associate with their t-shirts.

Now, here's your chance to be a good teammate and share. When we share something about ourselves, we empower others. We inspire them through this process. Do you have any collections?

Take a moment to share what you collect with others. You may be surprised what good could come from your willingness to share.

As always, remember: Good teammates care. Good teammates share. Good teammates listen. Go be a good teammate.

Targeting the Low Hanging Teammate Fruit
OCTOBER 10

Yesterday, I was walking with a friend and we were talking about a project I have been working on. During the course of our conversation, my friend used an expression to describe the strategy I was using to attack the project.

I was unfamiliar with the expression he used, but it captured the very essence of what I was doing and I immediately fell in love with it.

The project included a series of tasks—mini-projects within the larger project. I was struggling with how to handle the most challenging tasks, so I started completing the easier tasks first, even though they were out of sequence with the project's design.

My friend said, "Oh, you are picking the low hanging fruit first."

The low hanging fruit.

The beauty of having friends—teammates—who come from different backgrounds is that you get to broaden your awareness by being exposed to new concepts and new terminology. That was certainly the case in this situation.

Before I go any further, let me just state that I concede my ignorance. "Low hanging fruit" is actually a very common expression, particularly in the business world. I just happened to be unfamiliar with it.

I Googled it when I got back to my office and became humbled to learn of my naivety. So…if you're laughing at my ignorance, know that I am now laughing too.

If, however, the expression happens to be new to you, as it was for me, allow me to briefly elaborate.

The *low hanging fruit* is often used to describe the process of tackling the tasks that require the least amount of effort first. It's an analogy derived from the process of literally picking the more easily accessible fruit from the lowest hanging branches of the tree, instead of the riper and more appealing fruit from the top of the tree, which require more effort.

Sales and marketing folks use it in reference to going after customers who will be most likely to buy what they are selling, as opposed to the more challenging ones.

Politicians are frequently said to be targeting the low hanging fruit when they take on less controversial topics during their time in office.

Sometimes we can become overwhelmed by the amount of things we need to do to make an impact on our teams.

You have a teammate who is underperforming and needs motivated. You have a toxic teammate who is challenging the team's direction and needs confronted. Somebody else is jealous of another teammate's good fortune. Cliques are forming. Etc. Etc. Etc.

And somewhere in the midst of all of this, you need to be true to your own commitment to the team and invest in ways to improve your personal performance.

How do you go about accomplishing all of this?

There is no easy answer, but going after the *low hanging fruit* may be a good strategy for getting started.

Make a few simple *good teammate moves* like giving an extra high five or an extra compliment. Go out of your way to speak to a teammate who hasn't been getting much attention lately.

Those actions are the low hanging fruit in the good teammate business, and starting with them builds momentum.

Momentum is what leads to the force necessary to take on your most challenging tasks.

When you start with the low hanging fruit, your momentum eventually devours the entire tree and soon there is no fruit remaining. The same holds true for devouring the things that are keeping your team from being as successful as it could be.

As always, remember: Good teammates care. Good teammates share. Good teammates listen. Go be a good teammate.

Circling: The Art of Disrespecting Time
OCTOBER 17

A few weeks ago, I wrote a blog about respecting time. Over the course of several subsequent conversations about this topic, a reader posed an interesting question to me: *Is it possible to have too much respect for time?*

The short—yet complicated—answer is...Yes.

I am the type of person who has a tendency to bend over to tie my shoe and think *What else can I do while I'm down here?* Although thinking like this may seem to lend itself to ultra-efficiency and the ability to maximize my time, it more often than not causes me to actually become rather inefficient and waste time.

As modern humans, we have become programmed to fill the static gaps in our lives. We feel a need to be constantly engaged in activity. Smart phones have certainly contributed to this practice.

If we are standing in line at the grocery store, we pull out our phones and check our Facebook page. If we are in the hallway waiting for our next class or appointment to start, we pull out our phones and check the latest headlines.

We try to fill the gaps.

A similar scenario often plays out in my home that we call "*circling*." It goes something like this:

I'll be working in my home office and my wife will duck her head in and say, "Are you ready for dinner?"

I respond, "Sure, let me finish typing this last email and I'll be right there."

As I continue to type, she doesn't want to "waste" any time, so she starts to fold laundry.

I finish typing only to see her folding laundry, so I start picking up our kids' toys.

She finishes folding laundry and now sees me picking up toys. So she starts to compose a grocery list.

I finish picking up toys and discover her holding a notebook, busy making what appears to be an important list. I don't want to interrupt, so I go back to my computer and start working on something else.

This cycle continues until one of us eventually yells at the other, "Stop circling!"

Of course by that time, we are now both so hungry that we no longer have the desire to make dinner, so we end up going out for pizza.

Circling is the art of disrespecting time.

Our attempts to not experience any "dead air" caused us to become inept in the management of our time.

In the previous article, I also talked about Lombardi Time *(*If you're 10 minutes early, you're 5 minutes late.)* Taking this concept to extremes can lead to the same dangers as circling.

As you continue to arrive early, you run the risk of inevitably wondering what else you could be doing with that time. Your obsession takes over. Pretty soon you rationalize that it would be better to try and accomplish some other task than to arrive so early and just be waiting. You begin to see arriving early as wasted time, and it can develop into a very slippery slope.

Ultimately, Lombardi Time isn't about being early and circling isn't about multi-tasking. And neither of them are about efficiency. They are about prioritizing.

Being fully engaged with your top priorities is a way of sharing your most valuable entity—time—with those you value the most.

It goes beyond the idea of stopping to smell the roses. That concept is more about your own feelings towards time. Prioritizing is about _sharing_ your undivided time with others.

The ability to successfully do so is one of the things that makes an individual a good teammate.

This morning, I saw a man pushing a stroller with a small child, while walking his dog. He was fixated on the screen of an iPad that was attached to the top of the stroller. The child was holding an iPad too, and was equally fixated on its screen.

The woman standing next to me looked at them and commented, "Isn't that a sign of the times?"

I thought to myself, "No that's a sign of disrespecting time." His attempt to multitask was causing him to miss out on a special moment that his child will never get back. One day, they'll both wish they could.

As always, remember: Good teammates care. Good teammates share. Good teammates listen. Go be a good teammate.

Seven Things Teammates Can Share Other than Their Possessions

OCTOBER 24

The willingness to share is a trademark of a good teammate because it suggests unselfishness. Teams have a chance to be successful when they are unselfish.

Yet the act of sharing is often counterintuitive. Giving up what we already possess doesn't instinctively make sense, and that is why sharing doesn't come naturally to a lot of people.

It is ironic, since we are taught to share at an early age. Share with your sister. Share with your brother. Share with your cousin. Share with your friends. Share. Share. Share.

Let them have a turn!

With that much emphasis on sharing, it *should* come naturally by the time we reach adulthood. But it doesn't.

Why is it that so many people continue to struggle with the concept of sharing?

The problem may be in their approach.

We work so hard to acquire things and that makes us reluctant to give them up. Perhaps we would be more receptive to sharing, if we looked at it from a different angle.

The concept of sharing is typically learned through the process of parting with our material possessions—our toys, if you will.

But sharing transcends just objects we can physically hold in our hands. In actuality, some of the most valuable sharing occurs outside of those confines, especially when you belong to a team.

Understanding that you are able to part with something and get something else back in return makes it easier to engage in sharing. You are not just giving, you are getting.

In essence, sharing becomes trading—a much easier concept to embrace.

With that in mind, here are seven things you can share with your teammates, other than your possessions, which will pay dividends:

1. TIME

You may not be able to physically hold it in your hands, but you can certainly share it. Sharing your time could mean lending a sympathetic ear to a frustrated teammate. It could mean doing something you are already proficient at for the benefit of a teammate, like playing toss in the backyard with your son. Or, it could mean investing in your own self-improvement. If you're an athlete, putting up extra shots or lifting extra weights is a way of sharing your time.

2. TALENT

What gifts do you have that someone else doesn't? Maybe you're good with technology and one of your teammates isn't. Sharing your talent with that teammate makes your team more efficient, and it ultimately allows that teammate to have more time to share with the rest of the team.

3. TRAINING

Sharing your talent is using your gifts to help somebody else. Sharing your *training* is teaching those somebodies to help themselves. How did you learn to become so good at it? Use those methods to teach your teammates to become good at whatever it is you are good at. Knowledge was meant to be shared, not stored.

4. THOUGHTS

If someone does something well, acknowledge it! Let them know what you think about what they are doing. Your praise, or even just your acknowledgement, may inspire them to do more. The same is true if someone is doing something you don't approve of. You may inspire them to do less. Keeping your thoughts to yourself can stunt your team's growth.

5. TRUTH

Sharing the truth with your teammates leads to respect. Even if they don't like what you have to say, they will respect your honesty. Successful teams are built on trust and that means sharing the truth.

6. TOXICITY

What? You didn't think everything on this list was going to be positive did you? Toxicity is something negative you can share, but you must be cautious to not do so. Whether you deliberately intend to or not, you can share your moodiness, your malcontent, and your toxicity with your teammates. That is why it is so vital to be a master of consistency when it comes to your mood, and to share your honest thoughts with your team…at the appropriate time and in the appropriate tone.

7. <u>TROPHY</u>

OK, a trophy may be a physical object, but metaphorically speaking, a trophy represents your victories. Celebrating your victories—your trophies—is a way to recognize those who contributed to your success. No one attains success alone.

It doesn't take wealth or skill to share any of these seven things. But sharing them will make you a wealthy and very skilled teammate.

As always, remember: Good teammates care. Good teammates share. Good teammates listen. Go be a good teammate.

Don't Let 'Em Quit
OCTOBER 31

If you have read my book *Building Good Teammates*, you are aware of my love/hate relationship with youth sports.

In many, many, many ways they are the home of everything that is pure and wholesome about the sports world. They are where aspiring athletes learn the fundamentals and get to experience the joys of being part of a team.

Unfortunately, they are also the birthplace of some of the worst elements of sports.

Recently, I was walking in a park and came across a field where dozens of kids were participating in a youth football game. I stood and watched for a few minutes when I happened to overhear a conversation between a pair of angry parents.

I found the topic of their conversation to be unsettling.

The mother was upset with the coach because her son wasn't getting enough playing time at the "good" positions.

As the game ended and she began folding up her chair, she laid out her rationale for allowing her son to quit (*Life is short, you are only a kid once, there are other things to do, etc.).* From what I could ascertain, her son had been growing increasingly frustrated and had consequently been asking for her permission to quit the team.

His mother said that after the way that day's game went she was going to let him quit.

The other parent responded, "I don't blame you at all."

From years of sitting in bleachers, recruiting, scouting, and just watching games as an emotionally-detached observer, I can state with sincerity that wasn't the first time I have overheard a conversation of that nature. Yet every time I hear one, I cringe.

Unlike the other parent, I _do_ blame you for allowing your child to quit. Let me clarify...

I don't blame you as a parent for feeling frustrated. You may be right. Your child might not be getting a fair opportunity.

Coaches are human and subject to succumbing to the entire gamut of human emotions and faults.

For a variety of reasons, coaches can sometimes become enamored with certain players, and that can cause them to overlook the value of the other players on the team, including your child. The coach might be playing favorites— intentionally or unintentionally.

You might also be wrong.

As parents, we only get to see a small portion of our child's involvement with the team—the tip of the proverbial iceberg, if you will. We aren't always privy to what and how our child is doing in practices. Coaches interact with players far more frequently in practices than they do in the games.

Players establish dependability and typically attain the coach's trust based on how they perform in practices. Your child may not have been successful at doing those things in that setting.

Being right or wrong, justified or unjustified, in your frustrations has nothing to do with why you as a parent are to blame.

You are to blame because all of the bad that will inevitably come from giving your child permission to quit mid-season will be your fault. You will have planted a seed in him or her that says when things get tough, when things are frustrating, and when conditions are less than ideal, it's OK to just quit.

Life can be tough. Life can be frustrating. And the conditions in life are rarely ideal.

Sports are an opportunity to teach life and to prepare kids for what life may have in store for them.

The "wanting to quit" situation can be a teachable moment. The problem is that too many parents miss out on this opportunity because they are sidetracked by their own emotional connection to the situation.

For the teachable moment to work, there has to be a shift in the parents' perspective. Instead of focusing on your child's stats, role, playing time, or even the score, you should focus on your child's resiliency.

Let your child know how proud you are of their determination and commitment. Let them know how much you respect their willingness to stick with something that is challenging for them.

When their games are over, don't talk about the outcome or their involvement in the game. Just tell them that you enjoyed coming to their game.

Taking this approach will pay dividends beyond your wildest dreams. It will set your child up for success in life. And if you're lucky enough, your shift in approach might just teach your child to be a good teammate.

The amount of points they score, tackles they make, or goals they stop won't play a role in the level of happiness they find in their adult life. But learning to be a good teammate most certainly will.

Don't let 'em quit.

As always, remember: Good teammates care. Good teammates share. Good teammates listen. Go be a good teammate.

Coach I's Impact
NOVEMBER 7

File this under the heading *Why we teach.*

I got a message a few days ago from a former classmate, letting me know his father was going to be celebrating a milestone birthday this week.

His father, Tom Iagulli, was a beloved teacher and coach at our school. Everyone adored Mr. Iagulli, and I consider myself very fortunate to have been in his eighth grade English class.

He was more commonly known as "Mr. I" or "Coach I"—which couldn't be more ironic, since there was nothing "I" about him. He was entirely *we, us,* and *our* and perhaps the most unselfish man I've ever met.

As a teacher, he was gifted beyond measure. Think Robin Williams' character in *Dead Poet's Society*, only way more dynamic.

Mr. I had a knack for captivating his students' attention and inspiring them to think big. He made Shakespeare and books like *The Pigman, Fahrenheit 451*, and *Jonathan Livingston*

Seagull seem cool to too-cool-for-school seventh and eighth graders.

It takes a special person to be able to tame that age group. Mr. I did it with ease.

When I think of the impact he had on me, I smile. There is barely an aspect of my life that Mr. I didn't play a role in shaping.

As a coach, I wanted to be him.

As a professional speaker, I make use of the same techniques I learned in his speech class all of the time. Great teachers have a way of making us remember the fundamentals.

As an author and blogger, I routinely think about the things I learned in his English class. I think about him teaching me the importance of *power writing*, grammar, and syntax. *(Right now, I'm thinking about whether or not he would approve of my use of such a nondescript word as "things" in the first sentence of this paragraph!)*

Some of the most valuable lessons I learned from Mr. I came from outside the classroom and off the field, like the importance of integrity, commitment, and loyalty. He embodied what it meant to be a good parent and a devoted husband. I've tried my best to follow his example to be both.

The hardest part about being a teacher, or a coach, or a mentor of any kind is that we don't always get to see an immediate return on our investment. It can take years to see the fruits of our labor come to fruition and the realization of the impact we had on a student.

As one life goes on to impact another, the really hard part is coming to grips with the fact that we may not live long enough to see the depth and breadth of the ripple effect brought on by our efforts.

If you are a teacher, or a coach, or a mentor...or even a parent, don't let this deferment period discourage you—teach anyway.

Teach because you have the chance to impact. Teach because you have the chance to inspire. Teach because you have the chance to fill the void in a child's life. Teach because you have the chance to initiate the next ripple and become the Mr. I in someone's story.

When I graduated high school, Mr. I gave me a hardback copy of *Jonathan Livingston Seagull*. I have hundreds of books on the shelves in my office, but that one is special. I keep it locked away in my safe with my other important possessions.

On the inside cover of the book, Mr. I wrote the following:

"I just want you to know that when you "fly away," sometime in the middle of here and now we'll meet. And I do so look forward to having you teach me a thing or two!!!"

It is a reference to a passage in the book that we studied in his class. It is also insight into the mindset of a great teacher.

I doubt I will ever attain a level of wisdom that will render me capable of actually teaching Mr. I "a thing or two." But I continue to work towards doing so every day because I don't want to let him down. I strive to be a better person and reach the potential he saw in me.

As I write this, I wonder...Did I ever really tell him thank you? Did I ever let him know how much I appreciate all that he did for me and the impact he has had on my life?

I suspect each and every one of you has had a teacher, coach, or mentor who impacted your life the way Mr. I impacted mine. Make today the day you decide to be a good teammate and reach out to that person. Share your memories. Let him or her know you appreciate the difference he or she made in your life.

I assure you, they will be grateful for your gesture and it will play a part in them finding solace in knowing it was all worth it.

To Mr. I, happy birthday and a very heartfelt thank you. I hope you know that you continue to make a difference.

As always, remember: Good teammates care. Good teammates share. Good teammates listen. Go be a good teammate.

Lost and Found: Insight from Kendrick Perkins
NOVEMBER 14

As many of you are aware, I've been working on my next book. It is about the art of being a good teammate and shifting your focus from me to we.

During the course of my research for the book, Kendrick Perkins' name keeps coming up. Last week, I had a chance to sit down and chat with the NBA veteran and gain some valuable insight into the mindset of a renowned good teammate.

I realize that not everyone who reads my blog is a diehard sports fan, and some of you may therefore not recognize the name.

Kendrick Perkins, or "Perk" as he is often more affectionately known, has been a common denominator on some of the most successful teams in the NBA over the past decade.

He was a key component of the Boston Celtics' 2008 World Championship team. He also played a role in helping the Oklahoma City Thunder (2012) and Cleveland Cavaliers (2015) reach the NBA Finals.

The 6'10" center has been a respected teammate of several future Hall of Famers, including LeBron James, Kevin Garnett, and Kevin Durant—all of whom have publicly made note of the unique value he brought to their respective teams.

A *Sports Illustrated: The Crossover* article titled "Oral History: Kendrick Perkins, the NBA's Best Teammate" quoted reigning league MVP Russell Westbrook as saying Perkins is "the type of guy that's willing to do whatever it takes to help your teammates."

While you will have to wait for the release of my next book to gain access to the full insight of what I learned from my discussion with Perkins, I will share one tidbit that he gave me, to which I've become particularly fixated.

I asked him what specifically he thought his good teammate "superpower" was, and he described being able to "lose myself in the team."

Lose myself in the team.

Think about that. We live in a society where people are always trying to find themselves. When you consider the growing opioid epidemic and all of the other afflictions affecting our society, it would seem as though many of us are trying to find ourselves by looking in the wrong places.

As Perkins points out, the key to being a good teammate, and ultimately acquiring happiness in life, isn't finding yourself, it's losing yourself…in your team.

It's setting your ego aside and settling into the role your team requires of you. It's serving the needs of your team.

I prefer to conduct face-to-face interviews when I am doing research. I like to see the passion in the other person's eyes and hear the sincerity in their voice. I noticed both of those when I spoke to Kendrick Perkins about this topic.

It's hard not to be inspired by his unwavering commitment to being a good teammate, regardless of his surroundings or his situation. I think we could all learn something from this big man, with the even bigger heart.

As always, remember: Good teammates care. Good teammates share. Good teammates listen. Go be a good teammate.

The Thankful Teammate
NOVEMBER 21

The Thanksgiving holiday descends upon America this week. Beyond eating and drinking our fill, it is also supposed to be an occasion to reflect on that for which we are thankful and—ideally—openly express our gratitude towards those for whom we are thankful.

Being grateful is good, but letting others know you are grateful by conveying your gratitude is better.

The expression "attitude of gratitude" seems to have become and overused cliché. Yet it is nevertheless something that really good teammates have. They are genuinely grateful and don't hesitate to convey their appreciation.

In this spirit, I would like to take the opportunity to thank all of you for your continued interest in the *Be A Good Teammate* project.

Every time you open an email from us, click on our website, share our Facebook post, or retweet something from our Twitter feed, you help us grow.

I believe what we are doing with this message is making a positive difference in a lot of lives. I witness people changing the way they see themselves in the context of being someone's teammate instead of just an individual every day.

The message is putting a dent in school bullying. It's playing a role in reducing the opioid epidemic. And it is helping schools, organizations, companies, and teams everywhere become more efficient. We all benefit from these things happening.

Your follow, retweet, like, or share may seem like a small gesture to you, but it is important to us because it helps us navigate social media's mysterious algorithms and extend the reach of our audience. The more likes, shares, and retweets we get, the more people we reach...the more lives we change.

So from the very, very bottom of my heart, thank you for helping us grow and please continue to share the message.

I wish you all a blessed Thanksgiving holiday.

As always, remember: Good teammates care. Good teammates share. Good teammates listen. Go be a good teammate.

Wondermates
NOVEMBER 28

Let me begin by making it clear this is not a movie review—
an endorsement perhaps, but not a review.

I had the pleasure of seeing the movie *Wonder* last week
and found it to be both entertaining and incredibly inspiring.

The movie is based on R.J. Palacio's best-selling novel by
the same name. It is the story of Auggie Pullman, a fifth
grader who suffers from facial deformities related to Treacher
Collins syndrome, and his attempt to attend a mainstream
school for the first time in his life.

In previous blogs, I have written about the significance of
good teammate moves—those small sacrifices we make for our
teammates and the gestures of kindness we extend to them.
Sometimes we underestimate how impactful our seemingly
small gestures can be to the recipient. *Wonder* is filled with
fantastic illustrations of good teammate moves.

However, there is one scene in particular that I feel really
captures how powerful a good teammate move can be.

Auggie, bullied and ostracized, finds himself eating alone
in the school's cafeteria. It is a very sad and emotional scene.

The other students are either deliberately ignoring him or hurling not too subtle insults at him. But then a courageous little girl by the name of Summer stands up and carries her lunch tray over to Auggie's table and sits down.

Her good teammate move changes everything. Auggie starts to like school. The other kids become accepting of him and start to see beyond his physical deformities. Summer's gesture initiates an entire shift in the culture of their school.

She is an example of an especially important type of good teammate I call the *"wondermate."*

People always cite the *wonders* of teamwork (efficiency, synergy, productivity, etc.), but genuine teamwork doesn't happen without good teammates. And having a team full of good teammates rarely happens without the emergence of the wondermate.

The wondermate is that first teammate who demonstrates the courage needed to stand up and initiate change. The wondermate is the first person to take action.

They are the ones who inspire other good teammates to get onboard and join the movement. Without wondermates, the wonders of teamwork never happen.

Is it leadership? Maybe. Is it being a good teammate? Absolutely.

If you are looking for change on your team, be on the lookout for the wondermate. But be careful, the wondermate you're looking for may be you.

As always, remember: Good teammates care. Good teammates share. Good teammates listen. Go be a good teammate.

Three Rules of
Good Teammate Communication
DECEMBER 5

Communication is an essential component of group success. It doesn't matter if it's on the court or in the boardroom, good teams have good communication.

Everybody on the team is expected to convey information. We convey the coach's instructions to our teammates. We convey the boss's instructions to our coworkers.

But good teammates take it a step further than just conveying. Good teammates live by three *absolute* rules for communication. Their commitment to these rules is what allows them to minimize drama and be valued members of the team.

1. <u>THEY COMMUNICATE TO CONGRATULATE</u>

The word jealousy is so foreign to a good teammate that it never even enters into the equation. They are able to genuinely rejoice in the accomplishment of another team member, because they understand that when a teammate wins...the team wins.

Good teammates know that being generous with congratulatory comments strengthens the bond between members of the team.

Letting your teammates know you're happy for them builds rapport and prevents jealousy.

2. THEY COMMUNICATE TO CONSOLE

Bad things happen. Failures happen. When a member of the team is struggling, good teammates emerge to show their support.

Good teammates use their words to ease their teammates' pain and to get others back on track.

While congratulating and consoling are important, the third rule is critical and is too often overlooked.

3. THEY COMMUNICATE TO CONFRONT

When something or someone is disrupting the team's culture, good teammates communicate their displeasure and confront the source of the problem.

They don't turn a blind eye to it and hope it will go away on its own. They know it won't. It will fester and it will eventually tear the team apart. That is why good teammates choose to confront.

Sticking to these three rules prevents gossip, backstabbing, and, of course, silence. Nothing destroys a team or creates a toxic environment quicker than gossip, backstabbing, and good people not speaking up against wrongs.

Very simply, if it doesn't fall into the category of *congratulate*, *console*, or *confront*, don't say it.

It won't bring value to the team!

As always, remember: Good teammates care. Good teammates share. Good teammates listen. Go be a good teammate.

Amy the Balloon Lady
DECEMBER 12

Few of my blogs receive more positive feedback than those written about the good teammates I happen upon in the most unlikely places. People like "Darnell the Mover," whose work ethic and vibrant personality turned our moving nightmare into a cherished memory.

They are ordinary individuals who seem to go about their lives with an extraordinary amount of contagious zeal.

Last night, I crossed paths with another one of those inspiring individuals.

We were out to dinner with some relatives who were visiting from out of town when *Amy the Balloon Lady* approached our table. She asked if she could make balloon animals for our kids.

I have to admit I wasn't initially thrilled with her presence. I was hungry, tired, and just wanted to spend an evening catching up with our guests. But as I watched her twist balloons into the shape of a Christmas elf, I couldn't help but notice the rather large smile growing on my daughter's face, as well as the faces of everyone else at our table.

Amy proceeded to twist more balloons and then handed a purple unicorn to my other daughter. I marveled at her creativity and thought to myself, "This *Amy the Balloon Lady* is good."

She told us she could make over 6,000 different balloon shapes. One of the members of our party was a diehard Pittsburgh Steelers fan and challenged her to make the Steeler's logo. She promptly obliged, as we all smiled and applauded.

For the rest of the evening, I watched Amy go from table to table, twisting balloons and creating joy.

She eventually made her way back to our table. I commented that she seemed to really enjoy her work, to which she responded with a very rhetorical, "Is there a better way to spend your life than making people smile?"

Amy proceeded to tell us the story of how she came to be in her line of work. When she got out of the military, she found herself struggling to find a job. On a whim, she went to the Six Flags amusement park near her home in Chicago to see if they had any openings.

They told her they were looking for a clown. That wasn't exactly what she had in mind for employment, but she accepted their offer. During the course of her clown training, she discovered she was particularly good at making balloon shapes—and making people smile.

Eventually, she started doing birthday parties and entertaining guests at local restaurants on the side. After a while, her side gig grew so big that she left the amusement park and started her own business.

Amy the Balloon Lady embodies so many of the qualities of a good teammate. She is enthusiastic, passionate, dedicated, unselfish, etc. She is also a great example of the impact the introduction of a good teammate can have on a team.

I left the restaurant last night in a fantastic mood. Everybody in our party did. And it wasn't because of the chef, or the waitstaff, or the décor of the restaurant. It was because of *Amy the Balloon Lady*.

Our food was good. The service was fine. But the joy she brought to our evening is what made the biggest difference in our dining experience. Her attitude towards life was contagious. The restaurant manager who decided to hire her made a wise decision.

So many times, we are fooled into thinking that it is the rock stars on our teams that make the biggest difference. But that is not the case. The real impact is caused by the good teammates whose energy and enthusiasm inspire everyone on the team to want to be better.

Rare individuals like *Amy the Balloon Lady* are the real rock stars. They ignite our passion for life and inspire us to want to become better versions of ourselves.

Their willingness to share their talents and be an example of what happiness looks like are what propel teams to success.

As always, remember: Good teammates care. Good teammates share. Good teammates listen. Go be a good teammate.

Blindsided by Life
DECEMBER 19

Given the proximity to Christmas, I had intended to write a very brief blog this week, offering wishes for a safe and blessed holiday to all of our readers.

But I was reminded recently how quickly life can blindside us with unwanted tragedy, so I would like to instead share a couple of reflections from the events of my past week that I feel have good teammate relevance.

We lost a dear family member Wednesday. Dwayne was just 27 years old and seemed to have left this world much too soon.

As I spoke with other grieving friends and family at the funeral, I thought of Linda Ellis' clever poem *The Dash*, which calls attention to the significance of the punctuation mark that is often used to separate the year of birth and the year of death on a person's tombstone. (*1990 – 2017*)

It's not the numbers that appear before or after the dash that matter, it's what happens between them that tells the story of a person's life.

Dwayne packed a lot of life into his abbreviated *dash*.

He had a world class smile and an infectious laugh. In fact, his laugh was so uncommon that it was truly a gift. When he laughed, others were rendered helpless to resist its contagiousness and soon found themselves joining in.

I suspect he laughed and caused others to laugh more in his brief 27 years than most men do their entire life. Dwayne used his gift to bring joy to others and that added tremendous significance to his *dash*.

Good teammates use their gifts to touch the lives of others.

When the funeral ended, a few close family members made their way back to his parents' home. As we interacted with one another, the idea that *a family is a team* was reinforced.

In this case, it was a family of good teammates. They shared. They cared. And they listened. They provided each other with exactly the kind of support that was needed.

If there is a silver lining in Dwayne's passing, it is in his final gift to us—a reminder of the fragility of life. None of us knows when our time will be up, or when one of our teammates' time will be up.

That's why it's so important to let them know how much you appreciate them. How much you care about them. And how much you love them.

Life is too unpredictable to waste time being anything other than someone's good teammate.

Make an extra effort this holiday season to let your teammates—whomever they may be—know all three of those things.

May you all have a safe, blessed, and merry Christmas.

As always, remember: Good teammates care. Good teammates share. Good teammates listen. Go be a good teammate.

The Year in Review
DECEMBER 26

As we approach the start of a new year, we just wanted to take a moment this week to reflect on the past twelve months and the evolution of our *Be a Good Teammate* endeavor.

We've been fortunate to build a loyal following on social media. Our "teammates" have come to enjoy the inspirational thoughts we broadcast each day, and we have come to enjoy sharing the message. With that in mind, here are the posts from each month of 2017 that received the most interactions, impressions, likes, favorites, and retweets:

JANUARY
"The talent of being a good teammate is the most valued talent on the team."

FEBRUARY
"What challenges the team bonds the team."

MARCH
"The ability to get along is an invaluable, yet too often underrated skill."

APRIL

"You either help your team's culture, or you hurt it. There is no in between."

MAY

"If your objective is to find success, then your strategy should be to serve."

JUNE

"You learn from everyone one you meet. Sometimes it's what to do...sometimes it's what not to do."

JULY

"When it comes to gossip, good teammates must have selective hearing and not engage."

AUGUST

(*It was a tie!)

"Three things a player needs from a coach: 1. Someone to encourage me; 2. Someone to hold me accountable; and 3. Someone to model good behavior."

and

"Stop thinking lone wolf...start thinking wolf pack."

SEPTEMBER

"Good teammates don't complain about things they aren't willing to try and change."

OCTOBER

"Doesn't matter if you see yourself as a leader or a follower, you still need to be a good teammate."

NOVEMBER

"Good teammates despise laziness."

DECEMBER

"Good teammates contribute when others deplete."

We hope you will continue to support our *Be a Good Teammate* efforts, as we strive to inspire more individuals to become better teammates.

Remember: Good teammates care. Good teammates share. And good teammates listen. Go be a good teammate!

See you next year!

The Key to Keeping New Year's Resolutions
JANUARY 2

Alright...here we go! Commence with the New Year's resolutions! This is going to be the year you stick with it and see your resolution through to completion, right?

Statistically, that probably won't be the case for most of us.

According to data from the Statistic Brain Research Institute, only nine percent of Americans who make New Year's resolutions feel they are successful in achieving their resolution. In fact, almost a third of us abandon our resolutions less than two weeks into January (*https://www.statisticbrain.com/new-years-resolution-statistics/*).

Why do so many of us fail with our resolutions?

Perhaps the answer to that questions lies in the answer to another question: *Why are you making the resolution?*

Are you doing it for yourself or are you doing it for your team? That simple shift in perspective can have a profound impact on your motivation and your success rate.

If your resolution is to lose weight, do it for your team. Understand that dropping a few pounds will allow you to feel better and be more energetic, which will improve the quality of the time you spend with your friends and family—your team.

It's easy to quit on ourselves. It is much harder to quit on our teammates. We have an innate desire to not want to let down the people who depend on us.

I used the example of losing weight. I could have just as easily used quit smoking, learn a new skill, face a fear, etc. The same motivation of doing it for your team applies to all of them.

Ask yourself: *How will this resolution benefit my team?* And while you're at it, incorporate these three "teammate" strategies into your approach for achieving your resolution:

1. TELL YOUR RESOLUTION TO YOUR TEAMMATES

If you are doing it for them, let them help you! Having a faithful teammate in your corner, encouraging you to forge ahead when your commitment starts to wain can make a big difference. The same is true for having a teammate in your corner who is willing to discourage you from making decisions that will take you in the wrong direction. But your teammates can't help you achieve your resolution, if they don't know about it.

2. POST REMINDERS OF YOUR NEW RESOLUTION EVERYWHERE

Visual cues can be tremendously influential. Seeing a note posted on the refrigerator reminding you of your resolution to lose weight can prevent you from getting off track. It can also remind your teammates to help keep you on track.

3. SET SMALL INCREMENTAL GOALS ALONG THE WAY

Small attainable goals lead to big victories—and make sure you reward yourself by celebrating your victories as you attain accomplish those small goals. *(Think: Victory Cake!)* When you win, the team wins. Having your teammates involved in your celebration solidifies the resolution as a team endeavor. Few things are more fulfilling than celebrating a team victory with your teammates.

It's good to set New Year's resolutions. If you haven't come up with one yet, here's a worthy suggestion: Find a way to be a better teammate this year. The pursuit of that resolution will guarantee positive change in your life.

As always, remember: Good teammates care. Good teammates share. Good teammates listen. Go be a good teammate.

Three Things Students Need from Teachers
JANUARY 9

My daughter was actually excited to go back to school after the long holiday break. She's still in elementary school, and I realize that as she gets older that probably won't always be the case. But for now, her excitement for school pleases me.

While she was thrilled to be reunited with her "long-lost" friends, I couldn't help but also notice how interested she was in her teacher's reaction to her returning to school.

My daughter couldn't wait to ask her teacher one simple question: "Did you miss me?"

Every teacher in the world was bombarded with that question when classes resumed after the break. The best teachers didn't dread hearing it, they looked forward to it. They understood what their students were really asking was "Do you care about me?"

Not long ago, I posted a photo on Twitter and Facebook that listed the three things a player needs from a coach. I think it applies to teachers, too. *(Let's face it, the best coaches always see themselves as teachers, and the best teachers always see themselves as coaches!)*

If you missed that post, the three things were:

1. Someone to encourage me.
2. Someone to hold me accountable.
3. Someone to model good behavior.

When you provide your players/students with those three things, you show them you care about them—and you answer their question.

Young people need someone in their corner, encouraging them to forge ahead when the going gets tough. They need someone to cheer them on when they are on the cusp of a major breakthrough.

If they happen to get off track, they need someone to rein them in and use their misstep as a teachable moment.

And more than anything, they need someone to show them how to act when they are uncertain of what is appropriate. Young people learn more from our example than they ever do from our words.

Anytime coaches, teachers, parents, grandparents, or mentors of any variety provide these things to those who need them, they give the kind of gift that changes the course of an individual's life.

As always, remember: Good teammates care. Good teammates share. Good teammates listen. Go be a good teammate.

The Girl Scout Cookie Saga
JANUARY 16

Elementary schools are still some of my favorite places to visit. When I speak to students about the art of being a good teammate, I always try to explain to them that you don't have to play sports to be part of a team. Everybody belongs to some type of team.

If I am reading *Be a Good Teammate* to the kids, I pause at the part of the book where the reader learns that a family is a team, and so are the police, and the fire department.

I ask the kids if they can think of any other teams. Inevitably, one of them will shout out "The Girl Scouts!"

Yes! The Girls Scouts certainly are a team.

Last week, a girl in our neighborhood was selling Girl Scout Cookies. *(It is that time of year again—cookie season!)* I have a sweet tooth and find myself unable to resist those delicious treats.

So I bought a few boxes, and although they were clearly for me, I did my best to try and pass the purchase off as a *good teammate move* to help the neighbor girl's cause.

Interestingly, the history of Girl Scout Cookies is steeped in *good teammate moves*. In 1917, a troop from Muskogee, Oklahoma became the first troop to sell cookies as a way to finance its activities. The girls baked cookies and then sold them in their school's cafeteria, while their mothers volunteered as "technical advisers" for the endeavor.

Good teammate move by the moms to volunteer their time and knowledge. Good teammate move by the school to allow the girls to sell the cookies in the cafeteria. Good teammate move by everyone who bought the cookies. And of course, good teammate move by the girls to invest themselves into an effort that benefited their entire troop.

In 1922, an article in *The American Girl magazine*—which was published by Girls Scouts of the USA—provided a recipe with detailed instructions for estimating the costs of ingredients and the suggested price for a dozen cookies. The article was written by a local scout director from Chicago, Illinois, who thought others could benefit from what she had discovered.

Good teammate move by her to share her recipe and her financial suggestions. Her generosity launched the uniformity of the Girl Scout Cookies program.

As every good teammate knows, *knowledge was meant to be shared, not stored.*

To commemorate the 100th anniversary of Girl Scouts selling cookies, the organization introduced a new flavor—S'mores. That flavor is back again this year, and I can attest from personal experience that S'mores do not disappoint.

I doubt the girls from that Muskogee, Oklahoma troop ever envisioned their little entrepreneurial endeavor growing to be as big as it is today. But that is the thing of about good teammate moves, you never know the extent of the impact and reach they may end up having.

When you buy Girl Scout Cookies, you're helping mold the next generation of leaders in our community—*a.k.a. our team*. Proceeds from cookie sales fund experiences that prepare impressionable girls for a life of caring and sharing.

You're not just buying their cookies, you're helping them learn to be good teammates.

The next time you see a Girl Scout selling cookies, make a good teammate move and buy a box or two. You never know what could come from your generosity.

As always, remember: Good teammates care. Good teammates share. Good teammates listen. Go be a good teammate.

(*Information about the history of Girl Scout cookies was obtained from the organization's official website. You can learn more at: *https://www.girlscouts.org/en/cookies/all-about-cookies/Cookie-History.html*)

One Good Teammate Could've Changed Everything
JANUARY 23

Last week, a University of Bristol student took his own life. According to Sky News, he became the seventh student from the British school to commit suicide in the past 15 months.

The news is devastating the campus community and capturing the attention of the world.

It is sad. It is a tragedy. And, given the alarming number of deaths to have occurred in such a short span of time, some would even say it is an epidemic.

When individuals that young—with so much life ahead of them—intentionally "end it all," we are emotionally moved. Our souls are touched and our hearts grow heavy.

Not long ago, I was speaking at an event when a man came up to me afterwards and told me how much he appreciated what I had to say about being a good teammate. With tears in his eyes, he went on to tell me that his son had recently committed suicide.

The boy was being bullied at school.

His story brought a lump to my throat, and as I searched for the appropriate response, the man said something to me that I will forever remember.

He said, "All my son needed was one good teammate. One good teammate could have changed everything."

Those are very powerful words, and an important reminder of the impact a good teammate can have on someone else's life.

We never know how much others are hurting, or how close they are to their breaking point. A small compliment, an extension of kindness, or even a high five can make a big difference in their life.

In fact, it could make more than just a *big* difference, it could make *all* the difference.

Today is an opportunity for you to be a good teammate to someone in need.

We are never better teammates than when we are helping hurting people. And in the grand scheme of things, it takes such little effort for us to become invested in our teammates' lives.

As always, remember: Good teammates care. Good teammates share. Good teammates listen. Go be a good teammate.

(*Information about the University of Bristol suicides was obtained from the Sky News article *Seventh 'Suicide' at University of Bristol since October 2016* from January 22, 2018.)

Three Tips for Investing in Your Teammates
JANUARY 30

Good teammates are invested in their fellow teammates. What does that mean?

It means you care about them on a deeper level. It means you see their failures as your failures. It means you share in their agony and rejoice in their success.

It means you put your time, your energy, and your talents into helping them reach their potential. Their "outcome" matters to you.

An invested team is a connected team. Connected teams have strong bonds and high levels of loyalty. Connected teams achieve.

So how do you become a connected team? You invest in your teammates.

Here are three thoughts from Warren Buffett—perhaps the most famous investor in history—on financial investments that can also be applied to teammate investments:

1. "NEVER INVEST IN A BUSINESS YOU CANNOT UNDERSTAND."

Really good investors do their homework before they acquire stock in a business. They want to know its leadership structure. They want to know its financial history. They want to know its projected earnings.

The same is true for good teammates. They want to know their teammates' stories. They want to know what drives them. They want to know their likes and dislikes.

And just like in the financial world, good teammates understand the responsibility to acquire that information is on them. They don't expect others to just reveal important details, they strategically seek answers and ask questions before they invest their time and energy into a relationship.

2. "OUR FAVORITE HOLDING PERIOD IS FOREVER."

Good financial investors are in it for the long haul. Warren Buffet and Berkshire Hathaway didn't get where they are on the backs of short term investments. They expect their investments to pay dividends indefinitely.

Good teammates enter into a relationship with the other members of their team with the same kind of commitment. This perspective leads them to put extra effort into nurturing the relationship. Bonds with good teammates are for life.

3. "YOU CAN'T PRODUCE A BABY IN ONE MONTH BY GETTING NINE WOMEN PREGNANT."

Financial wizards know there are no shortcuts. The process of making a good investment takes time.

So does building a relationship with a teammate. If you try to fast track the process, it will come across as disingenuous, and it won't last. The investment you make in a teammate must be sincere and your efforts must be genuine. He or she needs to know you really do care.

As always, remember: Good teammates care. Good teammates share. Good teammates listen. Go be a good teammate.

(*Buffett quotes are from the MarketWatch.com article *The Genius of Warren Buffett in 23 Quotes* from August 19, 2015.)

Step Up/Step Back:
Lessons from Football Season
FEBRUARY 6

The Super Bowl brought an official end to football season.

Out of courtesy to our international subscribers, I'll rephrase: The Super Bowl brought an official end to *American* football season.

As a fan, I enjoyed watching the games again this year. I found it especially interesting that the two biggest takeaways from the season both occurred in the final game. And they both revolved around the concept of being a good teammate.

On the professional level, Philadelphia Eagles quarterback Nick Foles goes from uncelebrated backup to Super Bowl Most Valuable Player. His story is fascinating.

The Eagles starting quarterback—Carson Wentz—was in the midst of an incredible season. He was playing fantastic and was the odds-on favorite to win the league's MVP award, until he suffered a season-ending knee injury in the next to the last game of the year.

Enter backup quarterback Nick Foles, who just a few months earlier was all but out of the game for good.

Foles' story is a lesson in resiliency, persistence, and patience. But more than anything, it is a lesson in being a good teammate. Even though he wasn't getting any playing time, he humbly prepared and made sure he was ready if and when his team needed him.

When that time came, he *stepped up*.

Go back a month to the NCAA Football Championship game between the University of Alabama and the University of Georgia and a similar good teammate situation played out with Alabama quarterback Jalen Hurts—only he didn't step up, he stepped back.

Hurts had been his team's starting quarterback the entire season, and he had played well. With Alabama struggling offensively in the National Championship game, Hurts' coaches made the difficult decision to replace him at halftime with freshman backup Tua Tagovailoa.

Tagovailoa would go on to throw one of the greatest passes in college football history to give Alabama the overtime victory, and become the hero of the game.

It would have been understandable for Hurts to be *hurt* by his coach's decision to bench him. He could have been jealous of Tagovailoa's success. He could have even rejoiced a little bit when Tagovailoa threw an ill-timed interception late in the game.

But he did none of that.

Hurts demonstrated class. He supported his teammates. And he supported his coach's decision. He *stepped back* because it was what was best for his team in that moment.

There were plenty of camera shots of Carson Wentz showing support for Nick Foles during the Super Bowl. But

Wentz was injured and unable to play. It's a lot easier to be supportive under those circumstances.

Hurts was healthy and able to play, yet he appeared to be every bit as supportive of his replacement as Wentz was of his.

Hurts put the team ahead of himself.

Good leaders don't judge members of their team by an isolated lapse in performance. They judge them by their complete body of work. Things like class, leadership, example, past performance, and sacrifice all play a part in that assessment.

Good teammates understand this, and it is why they are able to step back when it is needed.

I hope one day, Nick Foles and Jalen Hurts look back on their lives and recognize the tremendous gift they gave everyone who watched the games. Their gift was one of example—an example of what it means to be a good teammate.

I think we can all thank them for sharing that gift with us.

As always, remember: Good teammates care. Good teammates share. Good teammates listen. Go be a good teammate.

One-Upmanship
FEBRUARY 13

As many of you are aware, I live in the Orlando, Florida area. It's a location that caters to tourism and is filled with *one-upmanship*.

If *The Mouse* opens a new attraction, you can be sure that *The Wizard* will soon be doing the same—only on a bigger, grander scale....and vice versa. (For you "outsiders," the terms *The Mouse* and *The Wizard* are Orlando-ese for Disney and Universal Studios.)

There is of course more one-upmanship in this town than just what happens between those two entities.

If a fast food restaurant on International Drive introduces a novelty like trash cans with lids that open automatically, it's only a matter of time before its competitor introduces trash cans with lids that open automatically *and* have neon lights underneath them.

If a hotel starts leaving towels folded to look like swans on its guests' pillows at night, another hotel will leave towels that are folded to look like elephants and other more exotic creatures.

One-upmanship can be good for business. The healthy competition can lead to innovation and a more diverse marketplace for consumers.

The idea of one-upmanship can be good for teams too—if it's handled the right way.

When the healthy competition of one-upmanship propels teammates to work harder and contribute more, the boundaries of team success are pushed beyond what they normally would have been.

However, one-upmanship can also destroy a team if the healthy competition stops being healthy and becomes toxic.

It's not so good if it leads to jealously or resentment.

Part of being a good teammate means walking the fine line between healthy competition and unhealthy competition within your team. And that is done by being happy for your teammates' success and understanding that their achievement has nothing to do with your achievement.

The race is never with those around you, it's always with yourself.

Don't see your teammates as competitors, see them as something that drives you to be a better version of yourself. Let them be the force that compels you to engage in a little one-upmanship with yourself, so that you are trying to top today what you did yesterday.

Anytime a teammate tries to be a better version of himself or herself, his or her team benefits. It's a way of sharing our self-improvement with our team.

As always, remember: Good teammates care. Good teammates share. Good teammates listen. Go be a good teammate.

When a Gift Takes You Places
FEBRUARY 20

I received a pair of emails over the weekend that I thought were worth sharing. They both dealt with the same subject, and with the impending end to the winter sports season, they seemed appropriate to mention in this week's blog.

The first email was from a basketball coach who wanted to buy copies of my children's book *Be a Good Teammate* to use as gifts for her team's seniors on their upcoming Senior Night. She wanted to know if we could ship the books in time for her event. I assured her we could.

The second email was from a parent who was the president of his son's high school booster club. He wanted to place a bulk order of *Be a Good Teammate* to give to every athlete at their school's sports banquet. He wanted to know if we could help him out with a discounted bulk rate. I assured him we could.

I certainly didn't intend, nor even envision, the book to be used in this manner. It was written for children. But seeing it used as a gift for older students has become a fairly regular occurrence, and I am glad that it has.

The reality is there isn't a Hallmark card for the occasion. And frankly, even if there was, a card wouldn't be as impactful. For about the same price, the book sends a more meaningful, lasting message than a Hallmark card, or most other traditional end-of-season gifts for that matter.

When I graduated high school, my friend's mother gave me a copy of the Dr. Seuss book *Oh, the Places You'll Go*. She wrote a short message inside the cover, encouraging me to explore the world and enjoy all of the experiences life had in store for me.

Like most people, I got a lot of cards when I graduated high school. I am sure they all had something nice printed inside them and most of them probably even contained money. But several decades have now passed, and I can't remember any of those cards or what I spent the money on.

However, I have never forgotten *Oh, the Places You'll Go*.

I often tell people I grew up in a very small town, but that's actually a misleading summation, since I lived quite a few miles away from the closest thing resembling a "town."

At any rate, that Dr. Seuss book inspired me to seek new adventures and gave me the confidence to experience the world. Its message was never far from my heart, every time I chose a life-altering direction.

Be a Good Teammate was initially written as a bit of advice for my own daughters. I hoped that if and when they reached a time in their life when I was not there to guide them, the book's advice would do so.

Its message is simple: You don't have to play sports to be a good teammate in life.

As recent headlines somehow seem to remind us, it is important to have good teammates in the world, and it is even more important for us to teach young people to think and act like good teammates.

If you're a coach or a booster club parent, can you think of more meaningful life advice to share with your departing athletes than "B*e a good teammate?*"

I can't.

Years from now, they'll likely recall that advice and be grateful to you for sharing it, just as I am grateful to the person who shared *Oh, the Places You'll Go* with me.

As always, remember: Good teammates care. Good teammates share. Good teammates listen. Go be a good teammate.

(*By the way, if you are interested in ordering copies of Be a Good Teammate *for your athletes, send an email to info@coachloya.com and we will go out of our way to help you.)*

It's Probably Not Enough
FEBRUARY 27

I had an interesting encounter recently with a high school softball player. My wife and I were out for a walk when we passed by a softball field and noticed the girl.

She was out there alone on the field, working on her game. Over and over again, she would hit softballs off a tee. Then she would gather all of the balls up in a big bucket and repeat the entire process.

I was impressed with her work ethic and inspired by her dedication. As we passed by, I gave her some encouraging praise.

She told me she was getting ready for the start of her season.

This turned into a conversation, during which the girl mentioned that she led her conference in homeruns and batting average last year. She said she was hoping to have an even better season this year.

I thought, "Wow! This kid's got ambition." So, I asked her what her goals were for this season.

She said, "This year, all I want is for my team to win a championship. I don't really care about the individual stuff. I honestly just want my team to win it all."

She had a look of surprise on her face when I responded, "Well, what you're doing probably won't be enough."

My perceivably pessimistic response clearly wasn't what she was expecting to hear. But what I said was true.

I explained to her that if her goal was to hit more homeruns this year, or to raise her batting average, then she was doing exactly what she needed to be doing—putting in extra practice time.

But to improve as an individual wasn't her goal. She wanted her team to win a championship.

By all indications, she was already doing her part to be individually successful. Certainly, improving her own hitting wasn't going to hurt her team's chances of winning a championship, but would it be enough?

What she really needed to do was to get the other players on her team to be invested in getting better.

Getting others invested in the team is usually what differentiates a good player from a good teammate. All it would take for that to happen is for her to ask a teammate to come to the field with her next time.

Not every teammate can be a good player. Sometimes, there are just physical limitations. But _every_ player can be a good teammate. And there is no reason the team's best player can't also be the team's best teammate.

Sharing your desire to improve as an individual with another member of your team is way to be a better teammate.

This encounter happened to take place on a softball field. But it could have just as easily taken place on the basketball court, in the weight room, in the classroom, or even in the board room—because it is true for all teams.

The next time you are engaging in some type of personal or professional development, why not ask a teammate to join you? It might just be the key to achieving future team success.

As always, remember: Good teammates care. Good teammates share. Good teammates listen. Go be a good teammate.

Ethan the Encourager
MARCH 6

It was "Dr. Seuss Week" at my daughter's elementary school. The teachers had planned a different theme for each day of the week, and Wednesday was "Word Day."

The students' assignment was to pick a word that was special to them and come to school in a way that reflected the meaning of that word.

Most of the kids chose the sort of benign words that you would expect from someone their age. My daughter's word was "princess." She dressed up in a purple Disney dress and wore a plastic crown.

One of her friends picked the word "blue" because it was his favorite color. Or course, he draped himself head-to-toe in blue clothes.

As we walked to school that morning, there was a commotion coming from near the crosswalk up ahead of us. When we got closer, I realized the source of the commotion was a boy standing on the corner with a sign around his neck. He was yelling into a small megaphone.

The boy was my daughter's classmate Ethan Tasior—or as I've come to know him, *Ethan the Encourager.*

His sign had the word he had chosen printed on it— "encouragement"—and coming from his megaphone were very appropriate phrases.

"Don't give up!"

"You can do it!"

"Keep up the good work!"

I was very moved by the sight of *Ethan the Encourager.* I asked his mother what made him pick that word, and she said he told her he just wanted to share some positivity.

I thought about *Ethan the Encourager* the rest of the day. I thought about how we, as adults, are sometimes too quick to write off the younger generation and are wrongfully skeptical of entrusting them with our futures.

I found the actions of *Ethan the Encourager* to be, well...*encouraging.* I am certain we are all going to be just fine when young people who think like him are put in charge.

He possesses an important trait common to all good teammates—the *courage to encourage.*

It's easy to remain in our comfort zones, play it safe, and just focus on ourselves. But as *Ethan the Encourager* demonstrates, there are occasions when we need to show others how much we care by risking the ridicule of doing something out of the ordinary, like hanging a sign around our neck while barking positivity into a megaphone.

When I returned to school later that day to pick up my daughters, I noticed *Ethan the Encourager* was still at it. He was handing out homemade cards to the other students as they exited the school with encouraging statements printed on them.

I didn't know it was possible, but this somehow seemed to make my heart smile even bigger.

I hope you will steal a page from the playbook of *Ethan the Encourager* and share some positivity with your teammates today.

I assure you, it will be worth it. And it will make a positive difference.

As always, remember: Good teammates care. Good teammates share. Good teammates listen. Go be a good teammate...*and an encourager.*

Ten Ways to Be a Better Listener
MARCH 13

Listening is one of the primary characteristics of good teammates. They listen because they seek the truth.

Sure, we can influence others through our words, but we discover the truth by listening. It is how we get to the root of the problem.

Sometimes, we can improve our ability to be a better listener by subtly encouraging the speaker to be a better communicator. Here are ten ways for you to be a better listener and improve the speaker's capacity to communicate:

1. MAKE EYE CONTACT

The best listeners listen with their ears *and* their eyes. Making eye contact forces you to focus on what is being said. It also reveals your level of focus to the speaker. A helpful hint I learned long ago is to focus on just one of the speaker's eyes, instead of looking broadly at both of them. This simple "ninja" trick has been amazingly effective at improving my listening skills.

2. NOD YOUR HEAD

Not only does this encourage the speaker to keep divulging information, but the repetitive motion also triggers a subconscious feeling of understanding. The more clarity and more details you can get the speaker to disclose, the greater your chances are of gaining genuine insight into their way of thinking.

3. PUT AWAY YOUR PHONE

Remove your phone and all other handheld devices from the equation. This will minimize your distractions and prevent you from being tempted to take a quick glance at your phone—which we have all become accustomed to doing.

4. SHOW YOUR HANDS

Similar to the previous point, having empty hands reduces the potential of being distracted. It additionally sends a message to the speaker that you are open and receptive to what he or she has to say and that you are not engaged in any other activity. In general, people are more apt to trust individuals when they can see their hands.

5. LEAN FORWARD

We speak with our body language, and we listen with it too. When you lean forward, you give the impression of being more engaged. Your proximity to the speaker is directly proportional to the intimacy level of the conversation.

6. MIMIC THEIR EXPRESSIONS

Sometimes this will happen naturally through the psychological phenomenon known as emotional contagion, but not always. When you start to mimic the speaker's facial expressions, you convey empathy. Empathy leads to understanding and trust.

7. DON'T INTERRUPT

No matter how great the temptation to interject your counterpoint into the discussion, resist the urge! Remember, the discussion is about discovery and getting to the root of the problem. To do this, you need to learn *what* and *how* the speaker is thinking. If you interrupt, you may never gain the information you need. Be patient, there will be time when the speaker is fully finished for you to state your thoughts.

8. INTERRUPT

While you don't want to interrupt the speaker with your objections, it is acceptable and even wise to interrupt with a short request for further clarity, or to simply let them know you are not sure what they mean. If you wait until they are fully finished to ask for more details, you risk forgetting your question. You also risk compiling multiple questions the longer they speak, and by the time they're finished, your list of questions may be too long to revisit.

9. PROVIDE A RECAP

When the speaker is finished, provide them with a brief recap of what they just said. It doesn't have to be verbatim, but it does have to give them an indication that you heard what was being said. Providing a quick recap instead of a quick reply makes the speaker feel as though they were heard. It also gives them an opportunity to correct anything you may have misinterpreted.

10. PAUSE

Before you provide a response, briefly pause. Think about

what was said and think about what you want to say. Your brief pause lets the speaker know you are absorbing what they said and not just spouting off a response that you had been holding in for the duration of the time they were talking. *(If you really want to make this pause effective, nod your head while you pause!)*

As always, remember: Good teammates care. Good teammates share. Good teammates listen. Go be a good teammate.

Resilient or Dreaming Big?
MARCH 20

Every so often, a post will come across social media highlighting "Famous Failures." Perhaps you've seen it before?

The post typically has several photos of famous people, accompanied by a few bullet points outlining the "failures" of their lives. They usually include Michael Jordan being cut from his high school basketball team, *Harry Potter* author J.K. Rowling being rejected by 12 publishers, and Bill Gates being a Harvard University dropout.

The idea is to inspire readers through the resiliency of individuals who went on to achieve success, despite experiencing failure in life.

These are interesting stories, and there is certainly something inspiring about people who were persistent and didn't give up on their dreams. But sometimes I find the "Famous Failures" post to be misleading, because they present the individual's failures out of context and don't tell the whole story.

Take the example of Michael Jordan being cut from his high school basketball team.

Jordan was only a sophomore when he tried out for Laney High School's varsity basketball team. It is rare for any sophomore at any school to be placed on the *varsity* squad.

Furthermore, North Carolina High School rules limited the number of players who could dress for a varsity game. At the time, Laney High School had 11 returning seniors from a good team. The circumstances made it a long shot for Jordan to be put on the varsity roster, regardless of his abilities.

His coaches didn't "cut" him, per se. They just put him on the junior varsity team with the other sophomores, because they believed he would get more playing time there and have a better opportunity to develop as a player. They thought it would help him more in the long run.

Obviously, it did.

Michael Jordan being "cut" from his high school team is a story that's more about ambition than it is of resiliency. It's a case of someone dreaming big and not being afraid to pursue that dream.

It takes some real moxie to be a lowly sophomore and have the desire to try out for a varsity team that already had 11 seniors. That's dreaming big. That's ambition.

The situation with J.K. Rowling is very similar. She may have been rejected by 12 publishers, but that is hardly uncommon for someone with her background. She was a first-time author with no following and no history of writing. Major publishing houses don't normally take chances on unknown authors.

But she pursued the big publishing houses anyway.

Again, her story isn't as much about resiliency as it is about ambition. Like Michael Jordan, she wasn't really failing, she was thinking big.

The capacity to think big while others see limits is something good teammates have. Rejection is not a deterrent to them, and it shouldn't be for you either.

Good teammates are resilient because they don't fear the possibility of failing. Their willingness to see beyond the safety of their comfort zone inspires those around them. It's their way of sharing their ambition and their vision with the other members of their team.

And by the way, Bill Gates didn't fail when he dropped out of Harvard. He was actually a very good student. He willingly withdrew from Harvard because he wanted to devote more time to a business venture he and his friend Paul Allen had been dreaming about, something called Microsoft.

Fortunately, they shared their big dream with the rest of us—their teammates.

As always, remember: Good teammates care. Good teammates share. Good teammates listen. Go be a good teammate.

Don't Be Empty, Be E.M.T.Y.
MARCH 27

Have you ever heard the key to success is surrounding yourself with the right people? It's good advice. But it isn't always applicable and trying to heed it under the wrong circumstances can actually cause you a lot of unnecessary grief.

When you are part of a team, you don't always get to choose your teammates. Sometimes the situation dictates that you simply have to work with those placed around you. Unfortunately, in our misguided quest to surround ourselves with the right people, we isolate ourselves by disengaging from teammates who we don't believe fit into that category.

We start to overlook teammates who can't help us advance our agendas. We distance ourselves from teammates who we think don't matter, like those who have a lesser role on the team than we do.

It is the kind of thinking that leads to cliques and elitism.

When you can't surround yourself with enough of the "right" people, you become frustrated. This eventually evolves into apathy and to you becoming emotionally numb. Your contributions to the team begin to falter.

At some point, you find yourself so isolated that you feel empty inside.

We've all heard the expression "Teamwork makes the dream work." But when you narrow your team, you narrow your dream.

The way to keep this situation from developing is to remove the "P" from your empty feelings.

The "P" stands for pride—or perhaps more accurately, foolish pride. Foolish pride is what causes you to see yourself through a misguided lens. It is what facilitates your false sense of superiority and prevents you from making a connection with someone you perceive to be lower than you in the team's hierarchy.

Once you remove the "P" from empty, you're left with EMTY feelings, which stands for *Everyone Matters To You*. This is exactly how good teammates feel about the members of their team.

Everyone on the team matters to them, regardless of the individual's role or his or her capacity to help them advance their agenda. Good teammates care about everyone on the team.

They care about the custodians, the housekeepers, the receptionists, the interns, the junior associates, the benchwarmers, and everyone else on the team.

Their willingness to care stems from their understanding that every team member's contribution matters and plays a part in the team reaching its potential. Team success comes from teamwork—which comes from the presence of good teammates.

When you care about _all_ of your teammates, and treat _all_ of them with respect, you'll create connections that transform them into being the "right" people, and you'll soon find that success surrounds you.

As always, remember: Good teammates care. Good teammates share. Good teammates listen. Go be a good teammate.

Mawmaw and the Royal "We"
APRIL 3

If you ask people who have had the pleasure of working for a boss they truly loved, they will inevitably mention how they never felt like they were working for him or her, but rather _with_ him or her.

It's a gift that great leaders possess.

In many ways, good bosses are like good teammates, because they don't speak down to anyone. They show respect for everyone on their team, and it's reflected in their tone and in the words they choose.

Recently, I had a conversation with an executive who was genuinely loved by his employees. Earlier that day, I had observed him interact with his staff. I could see that his staff didn't just respect him, they loved him.

This man was incredibly demanding of the people who worked for him and he held them to a very high standard. He was no pushover. But the interesting thing about him was that he wasn't perceived as being domineering.

I asked him what his secret was to creating that kind of relationship with his staff.

He told me attributed it to two things. Number one, he spoke to everyone like they were his *Mawmaw*. Number two, he spoke to everyone in the *Royal We*.

He explained to me that early in his career he was very driven and sometimes that caused him to be short-tempered with people who worked for him. He often spoke to them in an impatient and blunt manner.

In time, his impatient and blunt way of speaking to people carried over into his personal life. One day, after a particularly unpleasant exchange with his wife, she asked him, "Why do you speak to me like that? You would never speak to Mawmaw that way, so why is it acceptable for you to speak to me like that?"

He thought about what she said, and he realized it was true. The man adored his elderly grandmother—his *Mawmaw*. He would never be impatient with her. He would never speak to her in a blunt, mean-spirited tone.

So from that point on, he started speaking to everyone with the same respectful tone that he used when he spoke to his grandmother, regardless of the message he had to deliver.

He went on to explain that his newfound awareness led him to also be more conscious of the specific words he chose to use when he spoke to people. He realized he used the words *I*, *me*, and *mine* far more frequently that he thought he did.

He wanted to send a more inclusive message to his staff and wanted to be perceived as being more of a teammate to them than a dictator. So he made a deliberate effort to replace *I*, *me*, and *mine* when he spoke to others with *we*, *us*, and *ours*— the proverbial *Royal We*.

The origins of the usage of the *Royal We* are believed to stem from the belief that a monarch's proclamations are given in unison within the divine rights of being a monarch. When a monarch spoke, "We" literally meant "God and I."

Over the course of history, the *Royal We* has evolved to convey a much different meaning. It's now used by leaders to convey a message of inclusion, and when wielded correctly, it can be a very effective tool.

How we speak can influence how we think. Our choice in words can also influence how others think about us.

The executive confessed to me that his vocabulary transition wasn't easy in the beginning. But eventually, it became a habit and then it became his standard.

Here's a *Be a Good Teammate* challenge for you: Go one day without using the words *I*, *me*, or *mine*. Replace them instead with *we*, *us*, and *our*. Consider it a way of sharing your commitment to your team with your teammates—whomever they may be.

Can you do it for an entire day? How about two days in a row? Psychologists generally agree that a behavior repeated for 21 straight days becomes a habit.

In this case, a shift in the way you speak to your teammates can lead you to become a better teammate, and that is always a habit worth forming.

As always, remember: Good teammates care. Good teammates share. Good teammates listen. Go be a good teammate.

Can Gang Members Be Good Teammates?
APRIL 10

For the past several weeks, I've been pondering a philosophical question: *Can a member of a gang be a good teammate?*

The question was posed to me by someone in the audience at an event where I had spoken.

My initial thought was, "Yes, even a member of a gang can be a good teammate to the other members of his or her gang, if that is the team to which he or she chooses to identify."

But the more I thought about it, there was just something unsettling about my response. Could it really be true?

On the surface, it at least seemed to be possible. If gang members cared, shared, and listened, didn't they meet the basic criteria for being good teammates? And if so, did the parameters of the "team" to which they chose to identify with matter? Couldn't they be good teammates on a "bad" team?

I really grappled with this actually being a possibility. It didn't seem right. Surely, there must be something that would disqualify a gang member from being considered a good teammate?

I took a deeper look at some of the ancillary behaviors of good teammates, but gang members seemed to always meet the criteria and affirm the possibility.

For instance, one of the primary behaviors of good teammates is their ability to be loyal. If gang members hold true to their commitment to their gang and to the leader of their gang, they would seem to be sufficiently loyal and in compliance with the standard. Most gangs demand a kind of *Ride or Die* loyalty from their members.

I searched for more insight, and I spent some time reading articles and watching documentaries about gangs. I even went back and studied old episodes of the *Sopranos*.

Eventually, it occurred to me that the very thing gang members place the highest premium on—loyalty—is ultimately what precludes them from being capable of being good teammates.

Loyalty cannot be separated from the virtue of honor. You cannot be genuinely loyal to anything that compromises your honor. As the expression goes, "Loyalty above all, except honor."

When gang activity causes members to engage in immoral or unethical behavior, their honor is immediately compromised, and so is their capacity to be a good teammate.

Furthermore, their honor wouldn't permit them to tolerate dishonorable behavior from the other members of their team.

While most of us don't participate in organized crime or get involved in gang activity, we can still very much be susceptible to the same nullifying behaviors as those who do, when we allow our honor to be compromised.

This often happens to individuals who align themselves with cliques within their team. They don't always realize it's happening, but it is. A *clique* is just a nicer, less threatening name for a gang.

To be a good teammate, you must care about your honor, and be willing to share your allegiance to it with your teammates. Your actions must always reflect your commitment to your honor.

As always, remember: Good teammates care. Good teammates share. Good teammates listen. Go be a good teammate.

Respect vs. Disrespect
APRIL 17

What matters more to you, respect or disrespect?

I had an opportunity recently to speak at a juvenile detention center, and this was a confusing question for many of the individuals there.

In my experience, this is a group that genuinely benefits from hearing the *"Be a Good Teammate"* message because most of them have never thought of themselves from that perspective. And for that reason, they have often struggled to appreciate the effect their actions have on those around them—their *teammates*.

During the engagement, I did an exercise where the kids tried to narrow down what they valued the most in their life. Was it money? Was it trust? Was it love?

The overwhelming majority of them listed "respect" as their final answer. To be very honest, I wasn't surprised by that response. It is a common response for this particular demographic. Most of them landed in their present situation because of an issue they had with respect.

But whenever we dive deeper, we discover that their issue usually isn't with respect, it's with disrespect—or perhaps more accurately, *perceived* disrespect.

Someone said or did something they determined to be disrespectful, and they felt compelled to retaliate.

The "being disrespected" issue certainly isn't exclusive to juvenile delinquents. There are plenty of adults who are also susceptible to this pitfall.

I always find it interesting how some individuals feel entitled to respect.

These same individuals would never say someone is entitled to *trust*. They would argue that you have to earn trust. But they don't feel that way about respect.

My advice to individuals who are dealing with this issue is for them to be more concerned with earning respect than they are bothered by perceived disrespect.

Focus on working hard, being honest, and demonstrating integrity. Let your body of work speak for you, and don't allow yourself to be distracted by what someone did or said to you.

Your deliberate effort to exhibit respectable behaviors like work ethic, honesty, and integrity is likely to naturally lead others to develop respect for you. And if it doesn't, then they weren't worth your time nor your energy anyhow. Either way, their approval or disapproval won't diminish the way your increased efforts contributed to your team.

This is how good teammates think when it comes to respect/disrespect.

The great irony of the respect/disrespect issue is that we can control one of those entities, but not the other. Typically, our stress comes from us fretting about things we cannot control.

In this situation, we have complete control over what we determine to be disrespectful AND how we choose to respond to it. Comparatively, we don't have any control over whether or not someone else chooses to respect us.

Sometimes, a "good teammate move" is simply choosing to be above the pettiness of perceived disrespect. Don't allow your ego to get in the way of you focusing on the things that matter the most to your team.

As always, remember: Good teammates care. Good teammates share. Good teammates listen. Go be a good teammate.

The Pooh Bear Statue
APRIL 24

Sometimes the best lessons in life come at the most unexpected moments.

I've been juggling a few different projects this month, and the stress associated with those projects has caused me in many ways to be something other than a good teammate lately to the teammates that matter to me the most—my family.

In the hopes of *quieting my mind* and just catching my breath, I laid down on my couch Sunday afternoon and took a nap.

Among the things contributing to my stress was what to write about this week. I have been so preoccupied with my other projects that I had placed my blog further on the back burner than I normally do.

Without realizing I had done so, I must have mentioned this issue during one of my recent rants.

When I woke up from my nap, a small porcelain statue of Winnie the Pooh was staring me in the face. Attached to it was a yellow Post-It note that simply said, "For your blog."

The statue is one of my nine-year old daughter's favorite possessions. She was of course who wrote the note and very conspicuously placed the statue on the couch cushion in front of me, while I was sleeping.

The inscription on the statue reads: *Sometimes the smallest things take up the most room in your heart.*

I was obviously touched by her gesture and had assumed she was suggesting that I write about the inscription on the statue.

But when I went to give her a hug and thank her for her thoughtfulness, she asked me if I remembered how upset she was and how much she cried when her sister dropped the statue and it shattered?

I did not. I had actually forgotten all about that happening. My daughter went on to describe to me how much it meant to her when I glued the pieces back together.

With a look of innocence in her eyes, she said, *"When you are a good teammate, you do nice things for others, like gluing stuff back together, even if it doesn't seem like a big deal to you."*

She was suggesting that I write about that story and not the inscription on the statue—which I am now happily doing.

The inscription on the statue is meaningful and very true. It is certainly applicable to being a good teammate. But her words are insightful too, and they are wisdom forged from the perspective of a child.

I suppose, the moral of the story is that the essence of being a good teammate lies in the continual willingness to do kind, generous acts that may seem like nothing more than a small inconvenience to you, yet often mean the world to the recipient.

Those acts are called *good teammate moves*—and they are our way of sharing our talents with our teammates. The more of them we do, the better teammate we become.

As always, remember: Good teammates care. Good teammates share. Good teammates listen. Go be a good teammate.

Bring the Good Teammate Message to Your Team

Are you interested in bringing the "Good Teammate" message to your event or implementing strategies to improve the quality of teammates you have on your team? If so, contact Lance Loya at:

Phone: (814) 659-9605

E-mail: info@coachloya.com

Website: www.coachloya.com

Twitter: @coachlanceloya

Facebook: facebook.com/coachloya

Join the movement and sign up for Lance Loya's weekly *Teammate Tuesday* blog at www.coachloya.com/blog

If you have enjoyed this book or it has inspired you in some way, we would love to hear from you! Be a good teammate and <u>share</u> your photos and stories with us through email or social media. We want to hear from you!

About the Author

Lance Loya is a leading authority on the good teammate mindset. He specializes in getting individuals to shift their focus from *me* to *we* and discover genuine purpose in their life. Lance previously wrote the children's book *Be a Good Teammate* and the adult nonfiction book *Building Good Teammates*.

A college basketball coach turned author, blogger, and speaker, he is known for his enthusiastic personality and his passion for getting teambusters to become good teammates. He has inspired readers and audiences around the globe through his books, keynotes, and seminars.

When not speaking or writing, he is a loyal husband to his high school sweetheart and a doting father to his two daughters—who, incidentally, were the impetus behind his heartwarming children's book.

Also by Lance Loya

Be a Good Teammate is an illustrated children's book that teaches kids the importance of teamwork and the three undisputable characteristics of all good teammates. Good teammates care. Good teammates share. Good teammates listen. You don't have to play sports to be on a team. Everybody is part of a team in some capacity!

WWW.COACHLOYA.COM

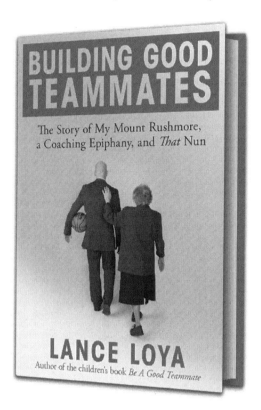